CREATING ROBUST VOCABULARY

Solving Problems in the Teaching of Literacy
Cathy Collins Block, Series Editor

* * *

RECENT VOLUMES

Creating Robust Vocabulary

****

Frequently Asked Questions and Extended Examples

ISABEL L. BECK
MARGARET G. McKEOWN
LINDA KUCAN

THE GUILFORD PRESS
New York   London

© 2008 The Guilford Press
A Division of Guilford Publications, Inc.
72 Spring Street, New York, NY 10012
www.guilford.com

Printed in the United States of America

This book is printed on acid-free paper.

Last digit is print number: 9 8 7 6 5 4 3 2 1

Library of Congress Cataloging-in-Publication Data

Beck, Isabel L.
    Creating robust vocabulary : frequently asked questions and extended examples /
by Isabel L. Beck, Margaret G. McKeown, and Linda Kucan.
        p.   cm. — (Solving problems in the teaching of literacy)
    Includes bibliographical references and index.
    ISBN 978-1-59385-753-0 (pbk. : alk. paper) — ISBN 978-1-59385-754-7
(hardcover : alk. paper)
    1. Vocabulary—Study and teaching. I. McKeown, Margaret G. II. Kucan,
Linda. III. Title.
    LB1574.5.B44 2008
    372.44—dc22
                                                                2008002158

About the Authors

Isabel L. Beck, PhD, is Professor Emerita of Education in the School of Education at the University of Pittsburgh. She has conducted research and published widely in the areas of decoding, vocabulary, and comprehension. Her contributions have been acknowledged by awards from the International Reading Association, the National Reading Conference, and the American Federation of Teachers.

Margaret G. McKeown, PhD, is a Senior Scientist at the Learning Research and Development Center of the University of Pittsburgh. Her research on reading comprehension and vocabulary has been published extensively in outlets for both researcher and practitioner audiences. Dr. McKeown is a recipient of the Dissertation of the Year Award from the International Reading Association and a National Academy of Education Spencer Fellowship. Before her career in research, she taught elementary school.

Linda Kucan, PhD, is Assistant Professor in the Department of Instruction and Learning at the University of Pittsburgh School of Education. In addition to vocabulary instruction, her research interests include classroom talk about texts and the design of meaningful and motivating tasks to support comprehension of text.

Preface

Readers' response to *Bringing Words to Life: Robust Vocabulary Instruction* (Beck, McKeown, & Kucan, 2002) has brought a marvelous period to our academic lives. We have heard from readers by e-mail, by snail mail, face to face, and several times removed. Although our connection to classrooms has never been too distant because we do research in schools, provide workshops for teachers, and teach teachers at the university, *Bringing Words to Life* has fostered a more direct line to exactly what teachers want to know. Along the way we have been praised and questioned. Although we have enjoyed the praise, we have been even more grateful for the questions, as they have caused us to think even more deeply about matters that we raised in *Bringing Words to Life*. And it's those questions that provide the basis for this book.

This book is not a new or second edition of *Bringing Words to Life*. Rather, it is a way of responding to the many interactions about robust instruction that we've had with so many individuals in our field. We learned from those interactions and eventually realized that we wanted to share what we've learned with our readers. In writing this book, we have tried to walk the line of adding to what we said on the one hand but avoiding repetition of the material we presented in *Bringing Words to Life* on the other. So let us apologize now to our readers if we have erred too much in one direction.

Beyond praise and questions, another part of our recent bounty has been teachers' anecdotes about their students' responses to specific words and robust vocabulary in general, as well as teachers' insights into aspects of their own vocabulary instruction. Below we offer several of our favorites from kindergarten children whose teacher had implemented robust vocabulary. The children's work was given to us at a national meeting by the director for literacy in Bridgeport, Connecticut, who wanted us to see how robust vocabulary instruction had affected kindergartners in a school in which 96% of the children received free or reduced-price lunch.

In the children's work that follows, we underline the target words—which we have to assume were made available, with the correct spelling, to the children—but everything else is exactly as we received this special gift. We had difficulty deciding which ones to include. Not only are they delightful, but the children's drawings seem to reveal a solid understanding of the words and how they might apply to their own lives.

The "comforting" and "intimidated" and "timid" drawings are so appealing because of the way the children attached the target words to feelings that we know are very real and strong for 5-year-olds.

In the next example we can't tell why the friend's house is intimidating, but we think that perhaps the use of "timid" might relate to the size of the grownup (perhaps the friend's mother) in the drawing.

Our favorite feature in the illustration below is that only the baby's face is visible, which we interpreted to mean that if you merely glance at something you may not be able to see all of it!

I glanced at my Ba-Be cUsin.

Look at how the drooping mouth in the "reluctant" example below captures reluctance.

I was reluctant to ride my bike.

And notice the satisfied smile in the mirror in the "vain" illustration on the next page, which suggests quite a clear understanding of vain.

In this book, we provide several more examples of the anecdotes that were relayed to us. They appear throughout the book as sidebars. We have attributed these to their sources when we knew them, but some came to us through second or third parties and their sources have been lost.

We have designed the content of this book around two elements that we found to be of keen interest to practitioners: questions about vocabulary issues and examples of instruction. Four of the seven chapters (Chapters 2 through 5) are based on questions that have come our way through e-mail, talks we've presented, and even a phone call from those who were at a book study group and wanted an argument settled. Sometimes colleagues have asked us questions that prompted our understanding that something we've said needed to be clarified. Two of the chapters (Chapters 6 and 7) provide extended examples of robust vocabulary instruction. By "extended" we mean two things. First, we provide full sets of activities around sets of words—activities that would provide a week's work of instruction. Second, we provide our thinking about the decisions we make as the instruction is developed.

Chapter 1, Vocabulary and Its Effects, is the sole chapter that is not structured around questions we have received or examples. Rather, we begin by setting forth our perspective on what we mean by "vocabulary" and explore some important assumptions that underlie our work. These pertain in large part to the relationships of vocabulary to comprehension.

Chapter 2, Which Words?, focuses on elaborating our Three Tiers perspective on selecting words for instruction. Chapter 3, The Basics: When and How to Teach, takes a close look at those basic decisions—when to present vocabulary instruction in relation to reading text, and the kind of instruction that is needed. In Chapter 4, Some Nitty-Gritties of Instruction, we take on a lot of smaller details that arise when considering how to develop instruction. These include considering such aspects as instruction at different grade levels and how to keep word learning going throughout and beyond the school.

In Chapter 5, What about English Language Learners?, we entertain issues of designing effective vocabulary experiences for students whose first language is not English, and the extent to which that differs—or not—from instruction for native English-speaking students.

Chapter 6, Extended Examples, presents two examples of developing a "cycle," or week's worth of instruction, annotated with our thinking as we considered issues and made decisions along the way.

Chapter 7, Professional Development, also provides extended examples, but in this chapter the examples are presented in the context of providing assistance to teachers who are developing instruction themselves.

Also included in the book are two appendices. Appendix A, Menu of Instructional Activities, offers an array of examples of activities that can be used as frameworks for designing instruction around specific sets of words. Appendix B, Some Well-Known Books and Stories and Corresponding Tier Two Word Candidates, provides extensive lists of wonderful reading for students at all levels and some recommended words to teach from those selections.

We hope that what we present will answer many of your questions about vocabulary instruction and its potential effects. Beyond finding answers to questions that matter to you in the pages that follow, we hope you also find new issues to consider and ideas that can enrich your robust instructional practices.

Contents

CHAPTER 1

✱ ✱ ✱ ✱ ✱ ✱ ✱

Vocabulary and Its Effects

Since the term *vocabulary* can be used to mean different things, we start by underscoring the point that our use of *vocabulary* means "learning *meanings* of new words." *Vocabulary* can also mean "words that a reader recognizes in print." Many of us have heard expressions such as "The children know the vocabulary in the first preprimer." That does not mean that the children have acquired the *meanings* of the words in the first preprimer—they already knew their meanings. Rather, it means that the children can look at these words and "read" them, or some might say "decode" them and others might say "recognize" them. In fact, the major goal of early reading instruction is to teach children to recognize the written version of words whose meanings they already know from oral language. The key phrase is "know from oral language." This is very important because learning to read requires children to understand that what they say can be written down and that what is written down can be pronounced and makes sense—that is, it has meaning. Thus, when young children pronounce written words, those words need to match with meanings available from speech. If text materials include words whose meanings young children do not know, a child might work out the pronunciation of a word and not have a match for it in his or her vocabulary repertoire. In such cases, he or she would get no reinforcement for being able to decode the words. Therefore, the goal of reading, which of course is building meaning, would not be accomplished.

The importance of being able to match a written word with meaning is demonstrated by Isabel Beck's recall of a beginning reader who was painstakingly working out the pronunciation of the pseudoword *reg*. The child, following a blending procedure she had been taught, said "/r/ /e/ /re/ /g/ /reg/ . . . *rag*." Although she had initially produced the correct vowel phoneme, when she put the sounds together she turned them into a real word that was familiar to her and said *rag*. Even more obvious was her blending of "fam—/f/ /a/ /fa/ /m/ /fam/ . . . fan." It appeared that what the child was doing was changing the pseudoword pronunciation into a word that had meaning for her. Subsequently when she was told before blending a letter string that the string

1

was not a meaningful word (i.e., "Sometimes it may be a pretend word or just part of a real word"), the problem disappeared.

An important issue, however, is that even though very young children's reading materials should contain vocabulary whose meanings they already know, this does not mean that they cannot engage in learning new word meanings. But this does mean that work with new meanings can and should be done through oral activities. In later grades, enhancing students' vocabulary repertoires involves both oral and written activities.

To reiterate, our focus in vocabulary is on teaching students new word meanings. But enhancing students' meaning repertoires is not an end in itself. The major purpose of having a large meaning vocabulary is to use it in the service of reading comprehension and writing.

HOW IS VOCABULARY KNOWLEDGE RELATED TO COMPREHENSION?

So now let's consider what we know about vocabulary and comprehension. First, there is a long history demonstrating a strong correlational relationship between vocabulary knowledge and reading comprehension. Davis's (1944) early factor analysis data, and its reanalysis by Thurstone (1946) and Spearrit (1972), showed that adults who score high on vocabulary tests also score high on tests of reading comprehension. Singer (1965) showed that the same relationship held for students in grades three to six. More recent results have shown that the relationship between vocabulary and comprehension can be demonstrated even earlier and more pervasively. For example, Snow, Tabors, Nicholson, and Kurland (1995) found that first-grade children's vocabulary knowledge correlated with their reading ability.

More recently, a number of studies have shown that early vocabulary knowledge is a powerful predictor of young students' reading comprehension years later. Roth, Speece, and Cooper (2002) and Catts, Fey, Zhang, and Tomblin (1999) found that kindergarten vocabulary knowledge predicted the reading comprehension of students 2 years later in second grade. Wagner and colleagues (1997) found the relationship to hold from kindergarten through fourth grade. And most startling of all, Cunningham and Stanovich (1997) showed that vocabulary knowledge in first grade predicted students' reading comprehension in their junior year in high school!

What can we make of this pervasive relationship? One way to think about it is to recognize that when children come into kindergarten, they come in with whatever vocabulary they have picked up in their daily lives. So, of course, some children will have less vocabulary knowledge than others. It would seem that being in school should boost vocabulary knowledge, so that the gap between those with lower vocabulary knowledge and those with higher vocabulary knowledge would diminish. But that doesn't happen. Students seem to stay in the same boat they were in early on, and one of the reasons for this situation is that little has intervened to help them change their vocabulary knowledge status. That is, very little attention is given to vocabulary knowledge in school—a situation that has been well documented (e.g., Biemiller, 1999; Blachowicz, Fisher, Ogle, & Watts-Taffe, 2006).

That little attention is paid to vocabulary in school may seem an odd thing to say since classrooms are full of words! Children are faced with oodles of words in many different forms every day! However, the kind of attention that is brought to those words—and again we are talking about words that are unfamiliar in meaning—is quite scant. As Scott, Jamieson-Noel, and Asselin (2003) noted in their observational study of 23 intermediate-grade classrooms, teachers spend "little time discussing the meanings of words" (p. 282). Rather, most attention to vocabulary involved mentioning—a word or synonym—and assigning—mostly words to be looked up in the dictionary.

Blachowicz and her colleagues (2006) note a lack of adequate attention to vocabulary in commercial reading materials, and cite the long history of this phenomenon, dating at least from Durkin's study in 1978 (Durkin, 1978–1979). Studies in the 1990s (e.g., Ryder & Graves, 1994) and more recently (Walsh, 2003) indicated that although nearly every text selection in a basal reader is accompanied by a set of target words, the attention paid to them is usually brief and is rarely followed up after the story. Fortunately, this situation does seem to be changing for the better in the newest materials (those with publication dates after 2005).

Although we don't know the extent to which the attention to vocabulary has improved *within* classrooms since *Bringing Words to Life* was published in 2002, we do know that, at the least, there is more realization that vocabulary is a problem for many students and there appears to be more attention devoted to issues of vocabulary instruction. For instance, vocabulary has been listed as a "hot topic" in *Reading Today,* the International Reading Association's newspaper, and it's frequently requested as a focus for professional development. Moreover, we have personally observed heightened interest and concern among teachers, administrators, and teacher educators.

HOW IS TEACHING VOCABULARY RELATED TO COMPREHENSION?

So it is the case that we don't know the extent to which vocabulary is getting attention in classrooms, but we do know that if attention *is* given to vocabulary development it *can* make a difference. However, not all vocabulary instruction has a positive effect on comprehension. Even instruction that seems effective at some level will not necessarily affect comprehension. The history of vocabulary research shows a pattern of studies, mainly in the 1970s, that succeeded in improving students' vocabulary knowledge as measured most often by multiple-choice tests of synonyms or definitional information. But most studies, although it was their major goal, found no effect on comprehension (Baumann, Kame'enui, & Ash, 2003; Stahl & Fairbanks, 1986).

As researchers sought to understand why instruction had generally not brought comprehension improvement, a theme began to emerge that suggested that in order to affect comprehension instruction may need to go beyond simply getting students to associate words with their definitions (e.g., Beck, Perfetti, & McKeown, 1982; Kame'enui, Carnine, & Freschi, 1982; Margosein, Pascarella, & Pflaum, 1982). This theme reflected a view of comprehension as a complex process during which a reader must act on information encountered in text to build understanding. The instructional implication is that in order to build the kind of word knowledge that affects comprehension, learners need to actively work with new words—for example, by building connections between new words and words they already know and situations with which they are familiar. It is these connections that make it possible for readers to bring to mind the word-meaning information they need as they attempt to comprehend a text.

Starting in the 1980s researchers began to develop instructional techniques that took into account the processing required for comprehension. For example, *semantic features analysis* and *semantic mapping* were developed to engage learners' processing by having students examine how words are related (Johnson & Pearson, 1978, 1984). Both semantic features analysis (Anders, Bos, & Filip, 1984) and semantic mapping (Margosein et al., 1982) instruction have resulted in improved comprehension. Another approach was the development of "rich instruction" that we engaged in with our colleagues. *Rich instruction* was specifically designed to provide explicit explanations of word meanings, multiple exposures to word meanings and uses, and opportunities for students to interact with the word meanings by discussing uses for them, making decisions about whether a word fits a context, and the like. We found that our instruction did affect comprehension of texts containing words that students were taught. These results were demonstrated in two studies in which we compared the comprehension of students who had and students who had not been taught the words (Beck et al., 1982; McKeown, Beck, Omanson, & Perfetti, 1983). In another study, we compared instruction designed to engage active processing with instruction that focused on practice of definitions. In that study, we also compared a higher and a lower number of encounters with each word in both the rich and the definitional instruction modes. We found that on a multiple-choice test, high numbers of encounters made a difference, but type of instruction did not. However, on measures of comprehension, type of instruction *did* make a difference, with the advantage going to instruction that both encouraged active processing of words and featured a high number of encounters (McKeown, Beck, Omanson, & Pople, 1985).

The conclusions of what kind of instruction is needed for comprehension improvement were confirmed in two reviews that analyzed features of vocabulary instruction in studies that succeeded or failed to affect comprehension. Mezynski's (1983) review of eight studies and Stahl and Fairbanks's (1986) meta-analysis of about 30 studies concluded that instruction that succeeded in affecting comprehension included three features: more than several exposures to each word, both definitional and contextual information, and engagement of students in active, or deep, processing.

WHAT ELSE AFFECTS
THE VOCABULARY–COMPREHENSION RELATIONSHIP?

A corollary regarding the relationship between vocabulary and comprehension is that although the relationship is strong, it may not always reveal itself. We have discussed how the kind of knowledge of words is a factor in whether vocabulary affects comprehension, indicating that shallow knowledge of, for example, a simple definition is not generally enough to help comprehension. Some other factors that may intervene are the density of unknown words and the role of the word in a particular context. Encountering a high density of unknown words might be like opening a textbook on astronomy and finding every other word barely intelligible. Facing a text with a high proportion of unfamiliar words will very obviously have a negative effect on a reader's comprehension. But readers are able to tolerate some portion of words in a text that are unknown and still comprehend the text reasonably well (Anderson & Freebody, 1983).

The role of a word in a text may determine its effect on comprehension. Imagine the sentence "Beth couldn't decide where to go on vacation, but she knew she wanted to be free from the brumal landscape." If you didn't know that *brumal* referred to winter, you would not understand what it was that Beth wanted to get away from. On the other hand, consider the sentence "Beth looked out on the frozen, white, brumal landscape." In that case, not knowing the meaning of *brumal* would have little effect on comprehension.

WHAT IS VOCABULARY'S RELATIONSHIP TO WRITING?

As we turn now to the relationship of vocabulary and writing, we begin by noting that in contrast to the abundance of work on vocabulary and reading comprehension, the literature on vocabulary's effects on writing is extremely small. The relationship between vocabulary and writing is intuitively obvious. One of the joys of reading well-crafted prose and poetry is an appreciation of an author's knowledge and skill in selecting words that surprise and delight readers with their precision, aptness, and overall good fit.

Word choice is often one of the features included in rubrics used to evaluate student writing (e.g., Culham, 2003). Corson (1995) suggests that it is the content of language, especially the use and diversity of vocabulary, that teachers look for when their students are communicating meaning. They do this believing, as Vygotsky did, that the use of words within a relevant context is the best evidence available for the quality of student thought. Despite the role of vocabulary in evaluating writing, however, there has been very little research into how students develop their vocabulary resources for writing.

The evidence that does exist in the literature on writing and vocabulary is not easy to find. In a recent analysis of the first 500 articles provided by the ERIC database in a search for the key words *vocabulary and writing,* only 10 relevant articles were identified. Of these, nine dealt with second-language learners. The other was an interesting dissertation by Moseley (2004), who studied two groups of eighth graders: one that received intensive vocabulary instruction and another that received both intensive vocabulary instruction and writing instruction. Although there were no significant differences in outcome measures, the direction of the data indicated that students who received both vocabulary and writing instruction included more target words in their essays. Moseley's results are similar to an older study that also taught vocabulary with a writing instructional component (Duin & Graves, 1987). One other study on vocabulary and writing was reported at a conference on vocabulary in 2003 (Scott, Jamieson-Noel, & Asselin 2003). The study was based on three classrooms where teachers focused on "word consciousness," which is an approach that comprises intensive instruction on specific words combined with attention to word choices in literature and encouragement of students to use richer vocabulary in their own writing. In a comparison of the three word consciousness classrooms with three comparable standard classrooms, Scott found that the word consciousness group used significantly more rare words in their posttest writing samples.

These researchers' findings also showed that including a writing component in vocabulary instruction did indeed boost students' writing scores. But it is hard to know from the limited research that has been done the extent to which the vocabulary instruction or the instruction in writing was responsible for the enhancements to the quality of the students' writing.

There are a few reasons that might explain the lack of research on vocabulary's relationship to writing. One is that most research on vocabulary development is not longitudinal or does not cover a long enough period of time to trace the potential effects of vocabulary instruction on student writing. Another reason is that a commitment to vocabulary instruction without explicit attention to the use of vocabulary in writing might not be sufficient to support students' use of newly acquired vocabulary when they are called upon to express their ideas in writing.

According to some researchers and educators (e.g., Nation, 1990), students have a number of different vocabularies including *receptive or recognition vocabulary,* which is understood in reading, and *productive or expressive vocabulary,* which is used in speaking and writing. If you think about your own vocabulary resources, you should be able to recognize that there are certain words that you understand during reading but that you would probably not think to use in your speaking or writing. The question of how teachers can support students in using the vocabulary that they are learning from the texts that they read in the texts that they write is discussed in several places in this volume. (See, e.g., Chapter 3, pp. 33–35.)

Our intention in including this first chapter was that it serve as a foundation for some of our positions and recommendations in the chapters that follow. Our understandings of vocabulary stem from a long sequence of research activities in which we engaged, steeping ourselves in the research of numerous colleagues, and pondering the kind of vocabulary instruction provided to students that might relate to cognitive theory of comprehension. Our broad view is that vocabulary knowledge needs to be deep and rich and imparted to students in energetic ways that encourage them to think about what they are learning. We hope that the chapters that follow will be useful to you in your vocabulary pursuits, both professional and personal.

CHAPTER 2

* * * * * * *

Which Words?

The question of which words to teach arises because, given the enormous number of words in the English language, all words cannot be directly taught to students. However, not all words need to be taught because a portion of the wordstock will be learned readily from informal everyday experiences. At the other extreme are words that are used so infrequently that it is not essential to learn their meanings. Within the two extremes, a major issue is which words, or what kind of words, are most useful for students to learn and thus should be given instructional attention.

In trying to get a handle on the "which words" problem, we developed the concept of "word tiers" (Beck, McKeown, & Omanson, 1987). We thought about three tiers—Tier One representing everyday, basic, familiar words; Tier Three including words that are very rare along with words that apply to specific domains; and Tier Two as the set of words that are more sophisticated than the basic set but of high utility for literate language users. The organization of words into tiers seemed to make a lot of sense to people. But we also found that we have gotten a lot of questions about the details of tiers. So in this section we take on issues related to tiers and choosing words.

* Why are Tier Two words so important for vocabulary development?

Our advocacy of Tier Two words as the center of vocabulary instruction has pretty much become our trademark since the publication of *Bringing Words to Life*. We have focused on teaching Tier Two words because of the role they play in literacy. Tier Two words are the words that characterize written text—but are not so common in everyday conversation. What this means is that learners are less likely to run into these words as they listen to daily language. The opportunities to learn Tier Two words come mainly from interaction with books. And because getting meaning from written context is more difficult than getting meaning from oral contexts, learners are less likely to learn Tier Two words on their own in comparison to the words of everyday oral language.

Getting meaning from written context is more difficult because written context does not have the same richness of clues to meaning that oral language does. When we talk, our intonation, our gestures, and the surrounding context in which we are communicating all give tremendous support to the meaning we are trying to get across. When we read, we are basically building context only through the words on the page. Since the supports available in oral contexts are not available, we need to work a lot harder to mine meaning from written context. This is in part, of course, the beauty of written language. It can be used to communicate ideas and contexts well beyond our personal experience.

The difference between the words of everyday language and those of written language is made clear by data from Hayes and Ahrens (1988). They examined the words in spoken language and the words in various forms of written language, from preschool books to adult books and newspapers. Their finding was that word choice in the spoken language of mature adults—and these were college-educated adults in conversation with each other—was on a par with that of preschool books. More specifically, they found that adult conversation contained about 17 rare words per 1,000 running words of talk. By "rare words" Hayes and Ahrens meant words that are beyond the most frequent 10,000 words in the language; some examples would be *alias, nation, fearless, stroll,* and *scorn.* Books, even those written for children, contained many more such words: children's books had about 30 rare words per 1,000, and books written for adult readers had about 52 rare words per 1,000.

Hayes and Ahrens's data suggest why it might be difficult for learners to move from using everyday language to being a literate language user. A term used by Corson (1985, 1995), "the lexical bar,"underscores that point and also suggests why learning the vocabulary of written language is so important. According to Corson, a barrier—a lexical bar—exists between everyday meaning systems—the words in conversations—and the meaning system created by academic, literate culture—book language. Academic success is possible, according to Corson, only if learners cross the lexical bar (Corson, 1995). So if students are to become successful in academic life, they need to be able to get meaning from text, which in turn means being able to build meaning using the more sophisticated vocabulary of written language. The sophisticated vocabulary of written language = Tier Two words.

✳ Are all Tier Two words equally important to teach?

No—there is a range of words even within Tier Two. Here it might be useful to introduce another concept that can help in selecting words to include in robust vocabulary instruction—something we call "mileage." We think of *mileage* as how useful a word might be in a person's vocabulary repertoire. Consider, for example, the words *potable* (a potable liquid is safe to drink because it does not contain harmful elements) and *potent* (something that is potent is very strong and effective). Both are Tier Two words because they are more likely to appear in text than in conversation, they are not the most basic way to express the ideas, and they are not words associated with a specific domain of knowledge. Yet *potable* has limited applications to situations and contexts in which there is something to drink. In contrast, *potent* could be found in many situations and contexts: *potent* could refer to a wind, a voice, a remedy, an idea, and many other items. Thus when choosing among Tier Two words, consider whether candidate words are likely to be met in a variety of contexts. Take a moment and consider which word in each pair of words below provides more mileage. They all come from a short section in *Charlotte's Web* (White, 1952).

> *twirling*   or   *avoid*
> *private*   or   *tunnel*
> *stealthily*   or   *merry*

It seems to us that *avoid, private,* and *stealthily* are generally useful words with wide possibilities of application. Students could encounter them in many contexts and have many opportunities to use them. On the other hand, *twirling, tunnel,* and *merry* have much more limited roles: although you could *twirl* any number of objects, twirling is not a conceptually rich word that needs much beyond a quick demonstration to communicate its meaning. *Tunnel* doesn't go much beyond labeling a physical manifestation or its creation—the verb "to tunnel." *Merry* is mostly restricted to the greeting "Merry Christmas," whose meaning is fairly transparent.

✳ What if students don't know Tier One words?

We talk about Tier One words as the basic words of oral language that need virtually no attention to their meanings in school. But we readily admit that not all students know all words that could be categorized as Tier One. Even though we know that some students are behind their peers in vocabulary development, we also know that all students continue to add words to their repertoires during the school years. It's most likely that this growth will be in Tier One words—because those are words students encounter on their own, either in informal oral contexts or in simple written materials that are targeted to young students.

Given that there isn't time to teach all words directly, our perspective is that precious instructional time is best focused on those words less likely to be learned independently: Tier Two words. However, there are lots of informal and brief ways to help ensure that students have opportunities to encounter Tier One words and build new ones into their vocabulary. We will give some suggestions about how to do that in Chapter 3 (pp. 29–31).

✳ Would a word that is Tier One for some children be a Tier Two word for others?

No, words don't change tiers depending on the age or knowledge level of a learner. For example, *glance* is a Tier Two word because it fits certain criteria based on its role in the language: it is a not the most basic way to express a concept (which would be "look at quickly"), it is a general word that can be found across types and genres of text, and it is more common in written than in oral language. Now, it is the case that *glance* is probably not a good candidate word to teach students in middle school since they will likely already know it. But that does not mean it is a Tier One word for those students. Even though it is likely to be known by these students, the word still occupies a Tier Two place in their repertoires—that is, it is not basic, general as to domains, and more common in written language.

> Renee, a kindergarten teacher in Jacksonville, Florida, wrote us about two incidents of vocabulary use that her students' families told her about:
>
> - After Dad said he was finished eating, his kindergarten daughter replied, "No, Dad, there are still a few *morsels* on your plate. Do you know what a *morsel* is?"
> - After the child told a rather fabulous tale, his grandma asked, "Are you lying?" The child replied, "No, I'm just *embellishing* the truth."

Similarly, a word that would be considered Tier Three might be very familiar to some learners while totally unknown to others. Take *ranch,* for example. Students growing up in the western plains might know that word early in life. City kids might find it unfamiliar. But either way it is a Tier Three word because its application is limited to a specific domain; it applies only to a large farm for raising cattle or horses.

✳ Why is *piano* a Tier Three word when it seems so easy?

Tiers One, Two, and Three do not necessarily correspond to easy, harder, and hardest words. Rather, tiers are determined by the roles words play in the language. If Tier One words seem easy, it is by virtue of their role in the language. They are the basic building blocks of language—the words of oral conversation, of everyday speech. But a word in Tier Three is not necessarily conceptually difficult. Tier Three words often have particular and narrow roles in the language. For example, Tier Three includes words from the realms of science, engineering, and economics—words that would be unfamiliar to many literate adults, and indeed conceptually challenging. But Tier Three also includes words that may be familiar, such as *piano*—because its use is restricted to the domain of music.

Even young children will add Tier Three words to their vocabularies as they build knowledge of the world. *Butterflies, earthworms,* and *chipmunks* are all Tier Three words. Such words are appropriate for young students to know—but do not have wide application in the language—and they can be taught through simple explanation or illustration. Thus, they are not good candidates for rich vocabulary instruction.

❋ How can I know for sure which tier a word is in?

In trying to fit words to tiers, you are likely to run into some gray areas. That may sound frustrating, but that is the way language works: it is flexible and ever changing. For example, is *pebble* a Tier One word because it is common and easy, or should it be considered Tier Two because it is a more specialized word for a kind of rock? Is *mailbox* common enough to be considered Tier One, or is it a Tier Three? You could probably make a case for these words either way. When these gray areas occur, move to considering which words will be most useful to students and worth spending time learning—it's that mileage idea again.

Let's move out of the gray areas now, and back to clarifying the tiers framework. An important part of thinking through which tier a word is in is to consider what we want students to learn about a word and what kind of role it will play in their own language use. Tier Two words are general words that apply across domains. Thus, in teaching Tier Two words, we want students to use them to talk about people, ideas, and events in their world. We want students to think about how a new word might apply to the words they know and the experiences they have had. For example, because of the way a classmate acts, we might decide that he deserves the label "candid." As we find applications for a word, we are building lots of connections that will make the word easy to bring to mind when students meet it in a text.

In contrast to our goals for Tier Two words, when we encounter Tier Three words that need attention, we typically want students to recognize separate particular instances of the concept. For example, when we teach *plateau* in social studies, we want them to be able to recognize pictures of actual plateaus as distinct from valleys, mountains, or plains. Prompting students to apply words to their own personal situations is not the goal for Tier Three words. Imagine focusing on the Tier Three word *revolution,* which might be important in fifth-grade social studies. After explaining what the word meant, asking for an example of a revolution wouldn't make sense. Nor would it make sense to ask, "Have you ever had a revolution?" The point is not to have students invent ways to apply the word, but to build knowledge about why and how revolutions have come about (or perhaps just the idea that the American colonists' fight for their freedom was called a "revolutionary" war).

Now let's think about some specifics for Tier One. Since Tier One includes the most basic words of everyday discourse, common objects are included in this tier. So *umbrella* is a Tier One word. Although seemingly clear, we realize that this guideline can get confusing if you happen to ask, "But isn't a piano a common object—and that is Tier Three?!" Here is the differentiation: *piano* belongs to a domain, that of musical instruments. So it meets a key criterion of Tier Three. An *umbrella,* on the other hand, is just an object. Of course, you could push it by arguing that an umbrella belongs to a domain of things to use in the rain—but the point is not to push it. Rather, the point is to provide a way to make some useful distinctions.

✻ Can a word be in more than one tier if it has different meanings?

Yes, for example, words can have both Tier Two and Tier Three senses. Consider, for example, the word *incubate* given the definition "to develop or change due to the application of heat." This sense would be taught as part of science—incubation as a process of bringing to development. But a Tier Two sense of *incubate* might be defined as "to cause something such as an idea to develop." You could ask students learning *incubate* in science class a question such as "What would it mean to incubate an idea?" Responding to that question would extend their thinking about the word, and perhaps about words in general. But note that it would not support the science learning. Another example might be *pinnacle*. In its most fundamental sense, it means an architectural spire, which would put it in Tier Three. But its meaning has been extended to a more abstract, metaphorical sense of a high level of achievement, such as someone being at the pinnacle of his or her career, which would be a Tier Two sense.

When we consider which tier a word fits, we also need to think about what the goals are for teaching its meaning or its different senses. Clearly, a teacher might have goals of teaching both a scientific sense of *incubate* and its general sense. But the interactions around the word would be different depending on the goal.

✻ What are high-frequency words? ... And for that matter what are low-frequency words, and what is in the middle?

First a word about the concept of word frequency in general. Usually when people talk about "word frequency," they are referring to a listing of words by their frequency of appearance in written language. The standard example for a long time was Carroll, Davies, and Richman's *Word Frequency Book*. Published in 1971, it was produced by examining a large collection of texts used in school through grade 12. Other similar resources exist, such as the more recent *Educator's Word Frequency Guide* published in 1995 (Zeno, Ivens, Millard, & Duvvuri). These resources list all the words from the texts they include in their corpus by the number of times they appear (their raw frequency) as well as at what grade levels. In the listings, every word form is treated separately—for example, *run* has a different frequency than *runs*. Even capitalized forms of words are treated separately, so if some number of sentences begin with *The*, that is counted separately from *the* appearing in midsentence. This also means that a word that has different meanings is listed only once. For example, whether *bank* means financial institution, edge of a river, or angle of an airplane is not taken into account. *B–a–n–k* appears one time on the list, and its associated frequency represents all the different meanings. In other words, there is no way to get the frequency of the word *bank* meaning a financial institution.

Okay, now to the question of high, middle, and low frequency. High-frequency words are easy to describe; they are the most common ones in the language—the ones we use the most every day. It is a bit more difficult to say exactly which words those are and how many there are, and even harder to say just which words are low frequency or in the middle. Several lists of high-frequency words exist. Although they have much in common, they differ in the number of words they have and in the specific words that appear. So let's describe what does exist and see if we can get a handle on this idea of high-frequency words.

Probably the most well-known source of high-frequency words is the Dale–Chall (1948) list. The updated version of the list contains 3,000 words that are meant to be "simple and familiar" and that have been documented as understood by more than 80% of fourth-grade students. The list initially contained only 763 words, many of which you would expect to turn up in simple texts for young readers, as well as all the basic function words, such as *a, about, for, of,* and so on. But the list also contains some words that you might not think of as simple and familiar, such as *glory, journey, gooseberry, morrow, settlement,* and *vessel*.

Another often-cited list of high-frequency words is West's (1953) *A General Service List of English Words*. This list consists of 2,000 words that were selected to be of greatest "general service" to learners of English. Although frequency was one factor taken into account in establishing the list, the words are not the most frequently used 2,000 words in the language.

Whether you look at the Dale–Chall list of 3,000 words, or West's list of 2,000, or some other list, they have much in common. That is, all lists of high-frequency words overlap to a considerable extent because they are meant to capture words that account for a large proportion of the words that are commonly used in both spoken and written language. For example, Nation (2001) estimates that the most frequent 2,000 words account for about 80% of running words in a broad range of texts. Although the frequency count comes from written texts, the statistic of 80% coverage for those 2,000 words most likely applies to spoken language as well.

Now let's move on to what's meant by low-frequency words. This label has a wide range of applications. It can apply to any word that does not appear on the Dale–Chall list—and in fact this is what the term often designates in the calculation of readability. Another way to think about low frequency is to reserve that label for words that are quite rare, as a way of suggesting that such a set may not be encountered often enough to merit instructional attention. Nation, for example, uses the label that way, describing them as "words that we rarely meet in our use of language" (2001, p. 12). But how rare is "rare"? Hayes and Ahrens

> Michaela Wilmarth, a middle school teacher in Providence, Rhode Island, wrote: A student "came to school Monday and said his mother had a party for people to watch the Patriots game and they lost. He said the party was a *mishap*! This is a student from my seventh-grade resource class for Literacy, and he is really excited about learning new words."

(1988) refer to rare words as those that are beyond the 10,000 most frequent words in the language. However, this would include such words as *cautious, edible, participate,* and *reluctant*—all of which would be expected to be part of even a low-level literate vocabulary. The main point here is that designations such as "rare" or "low frequency" are not at all precise.

Finally, let's consider what else there might be in addition to high- and low-frequency words. Certainly it is useful to sort words into those that are simple and familiar, those that are not useful to most language users, and those that are less simple but quite useful. This is especially the case when we are talking about written language. Although 2,000 words cover 80% of text, that remaining 20% can be very necessary to making sense of text. One take on this middle level of words is Coxhead's (1998) *Academic Word List* (AWL). This list consists of 570 word families that are beyond the 2,000 most frequent words, but occur with some frequency in academic texts from a variety of domains. The list was developed from collections of texts in 28 subject areas including history, the sciences, law, and psychology. To be included on the AWL a word had to occur in texts from more than half of the 28 areas. These words have strong overlap with our Tier Two words. And, of course, for the same reason: Tier Two represents our effort to identify highly useful, though not necessarily high-frequency, words.

✳ How do word frequencies relate to tiers?

Tiers One, Two, and Three do generally relate to high-, medium-, and low-frequency words. However, it is actually *differences* between tiers and frequencies that make the tiers concept the most useful. For example, consider the words *breaking* and *complicated.* They have about the same frequency according to Carroll et al.'s (1971) *Word Frequency Book.* However, we would argue that the two are quite far apart—in terms of their familiarity and their role in the language. *Breaking* is simply a form of *break,* a word that even toddlers are likely familiar with, and thus we would put it in Tier One. *Complicated,* on the other hand, is a rather sophisticated word, less common to children's oral language, and needs some explanation to communicate. Yet it is also a generally useful word for many domains and circumstances—from describing television plots to theories of the galaxy! All this makes it a prototypical Tier Two word.

As the above example suggests, we would not recommend relying on frequency lists as the primary resource for selecting words to teach, although frequency *can* be one useful resource for getting information on words to judge their appropriateness for a given grade level. Frequency lists can seem very tempting, because they are objective: they are gathered from actual data on the use of words in the language. But this very fact is also why they should not be relied on. Frequency merely indicates how often a word appears in print compared to other words in the language. That fact does not translate precisely into how difficult a word is or even how useful it is to a user's repertoire. As a further example of the eccentricities of frequency, consider a trio of words that have approximately the same frequency: *converge, decibel, moonshine.* Think about the differences among those three words.

Converge is a generally useful word and is a more sophisticated way to explain "coming together."

Decibel has a technical meaning pertaining to the level of sound. Even though it is a technical word, its general sense of loudness of things might be useful to students. But it would probably be found in a more limited range of contexts than *converge.*

Moonshine labels a very particular kind of beverage—one that is not frequently discussed! It is probably not a word that students have a general need to know.

❋ How do you decide which words might not be familiar for the students in your class?

The lens through which one identifies words to teach, of course, includes judgment as to whether particular children are likely to be acquainted with any given word. By way of exemplifying how that judgment might work, we'll take you through our thinking processes about five words whose role in a third-grade reading selection we'll discuss in the next chapter. (See pp. 19–21.) The words are *contagious, disease, prescription, sibling,* and *inflammation.* We judge two (*contagious* and *prescription*) as familiar to more third-grade children than not, and the other three (*disease, sibling, inflammation*) as less likely to be familiar. To reach our judgments we thought about the daily experiences children might have that are related to the words and searched our minds for any opportunities we have had to observe children interacting with these words. Our thinking was that many third graders have at least some sense of *contagious* through hearing about flu and colds being contagious, and of *prescription* through experiences of getting prescriptions from doctors and taking prescriptions to the drugstore.

We think that third graders would be less likely to be familiar with *disease, sibling,* and *inflammation.* In the case of *disease* we actually observed a fourth-grade class getting confused when discussing a social studies text until the teacher figured out that the problem stemmed from the students not knowing what *disease* meant. This is not surprising as everyday conversation includes the words *sickness* and *illness* more frequently than the word *disease.* Similarly, in everyday conversation the word *sibling* is much less used than the words *brother* and *sister.* And rather than use the word *inflammation,* people would likely use the words *soreness, swelling,* and *redness.*

It has been our experience that when teachers stop to consider which words their students may or may not know, they are often on target. Albeit we have had some surprises in both directions. However, well-thought-through judgment is a very useful component of good teaching.

∗ I've heard that children learn words in about the same order. Does that mean that words should be taught in a certain order?

The idea that words are learned in a certain order has some data behind it—but what does that really mean? First, it is certainly not startling that children of the same age will know many of the same words. This is because there is a set of words that all of us are prone to use every day in conversations. So children hear these words with great frequency and learn them. These are the Tier One words that are so familiar to all language speakers.

As children progress into the intermediate grades, they are required to do reading in which they will encounter unfamiliar words—many of them Tier Two words. The words individual readers meet will begin to be different—depending on what children choose to read. The point here is that children will learn the words they encounter frequently, and so if the same words are present in children's environments—be they oral or written—those are the words that will be learned. If other children are encountering different words, they will know and learn a somewhat different set.

Now let's think about what all this means for instruction in vocabulary. Even if it were the case that all children were learning the same words in the same order, it would not mean that words should be taught in a certain order. Again, order of learning occurs because of the words that learners happen to encounter. There is no need to learn words in a set order and no need to teach words in a certain order. This is because words are not related in a hierarchical way—that is, words of the language do not comprise an organized system wherein certain words precede others conceptually, as is the case with concepts in many content domains. For example, if a child understands the concept conveyed by the word *wet,* he or she could learn the words *saturate* before *soak,* or *drench* before *saturate,* and the like.

Words for instruction should be chosen using considerations of what words will be useful to students. The only requirement for teaching a word is that students already understand the concepts that make up a word's meaning, such as in the *wet* example above. If the underlying concept is understood, then rather sophisticated words can be taught. For example, the word *gregarious* may seem difficult, but if students understand the idea of a person who is very friendly to everyone and enjoys being with other people, they can learn and use the word *gregarious.* Simply put, students can learn words that may seem much harder than many of the words they already know as long as they understand the concepts that the words stand for.

CHAPTER 3

* * * * * * *

The Basics:
When and How to Teach

In this chapter we'll deal with two of the major decisions that need to be made: when to teach words and how to teach them. In terms of *when*, there are, of course, three possible places to teach words that are associated with text: before, during, or after the text is read. The question of *how* to teach ranges from parenthetically explaining a word to our robust instructional approach. We start with when to teach and then move on to how. But we'll meet some interactions of when and how along the way.

WHEN TO TEACH

✳ Why do you recommend teaching words after reading? What about preteaching words that will be in a story the students will be reading?

Our focus on teaching vocabulary after the story is a way to emphasize and distinguish two goals: one of understanding the story and the other of developing vocabulary. The primary vocabulary consideration for preteaching should be focused on which words need to be clarified for students so that those words don't get in the way of students' comprehension. Often with grade-level material there will only be a few such words. The attention they get before reading should be brief. The other goal is adding to students' vocabulary repertoires, which may take many encounters and a variety of information about the word. Thus, because it involves more than the story context in which the word is initially met, this rich information about individual words could interfere with the first goal: comprehension. The point is that the two goals need to be addressed separately: The comprehension goal involves simple clarification, the vocabulary enhancement goal involves elaboration. Trying to address the two goals simultaneously is likely to result in neither being well accomplished.

✳ Why do you say that just a few words will need to be clarified and why should preteaching of vocabulary be brief?

Given the redundancy of language, it is not necessary to know the meaning of every word encountered during reading. As we discussed in Chapter 1, depending on the role of a word in a text, readers can tolerate some unknown words without a decrease in comprehension. Preteaching should be brief because, as we noted above, the kind of elaborated attention that is needed for students to "own a word," including providing several contexts, may distract students' attention from the selection that is about to be read. For example, introducing the word *flustered* by explaining it means to be suddenly nervous and confused and then asking students whether they ever felt flustered when they had to talk to someone important might bring forth a wealth of personal experience. But such a conversation could well encourage students to dwell on their own or others' experiences with being flustered and distract them from the plot of the story as they read.

> When Margaret McKeown was working with a group of fifth-grade teachers to implement robust vocabulary, one teacher asked how to help students realize when words were and were not socially appropriate. The Teacher elaborated, saying she had received an e-mail from an irate mother whose son had used two of his vocabulary words to describe her "at a public gathering." The words? *Indecisive* and *crass.* Oops!

Moreover, when words are taught before a selection, instruction cannot take advantage of the text context in which the word is used. And, if too many words are presented without being contextualized, they may appear to be just a random set of words. Additionally, if too many words are briefly introduced before reading, it opens the possibility that the meanings among the words are going to be confused as students read the story. Margaret McKeown recalls observing a fourth-grade class that had been introduced to about eight new words before reading, including *obstinate* and *ingenious.* When *ingenious* was reached in the story, the reader hesitated over it, and the teacher said, "That was one of our new words—who remembers what it means?" and a student offered "It means he is really stubborn."

✳ How do you figure out which words might be introduced before reading?

We will use a chapter from *Ramona Forever* (Cleary, 1984) that was included in the anthology of a third-grade basal (Farr, Strickland, & Beck, 2001) to model our thinking about which words might be needed for story comprehension and therefore pretaught. First a synopsis of the story:

> Ramona, who has been well known to 8- and 9-year-old children for several decades, is about to have a new sibling. When the baby is born, Ramona is prohibited from vis-

iting her mother in the hospital because since she is under 12, she might have a contagious disease. Ramona waits unhappily in the lobby, and begins to worry that she might indeed have a contagious condition and, thanks to mind over matter, starts to sniffle, itch, and scratch. A doctor notices Ramona and she tells him her problems. He goes through the pretense of listening to her heart and the like and then writes a prescription that she is to give to her father. Ramona learns from her father that the doctor labeled her disease "siblingitis" and that the doctor had "prescribed attention" as the way for Ramona to get over "siblingitis."

The complete story has many Tier Two words. We selected four of them, as well as one Tier Three word, as important to comprehension of the plot and, as such, useful to deal with *before* reading the story. The words are: *prescription* (the Tier Three word), *contagious, diseases, sibling,* and *inflammation.* Below we show the context from the story in which the words appear.

Word	Story context
contagious diseases	"Children under twelve might have contagious diseases," explained the nurse.
prescription	[The doctor] tore off the prescription he had written [and] instructed Ramona to give it to her father . . .
sibling(itis) *inflammation*	[The doctor] said, "You have acute siblingitis." . . . "you weren't allowed to see your new sibling . . . *itis* means inflammation."

That Ramona might have some kind of sickness, *a contagious disease,* something that another person can get from her, is one of several ideas that is essential for understanding the problem that Romana encounters. That a doctor provided written directions, a *prescription,* to Ramona's father about how to cure her is salient for following through to the solution of Ramona's problem. *Siblingitis* is, of course, a made-up word that is nevertheless very important to the story because the doctor is trying to make the point (perhaps a joke) to Ramona's father about how her new sibling might cause her to feel sick. Thus, given the role of the five words in the plot of the story, it is important to make sure students understand them either before or when they encounter them in the story. Depending on the evaluation of how familiar one's particular students are with these words, we would introduce all or some of them before reading (see discussion of judging familiarity of words in Chapter 2, p. 15). Below is our ranking of likely familiarity for third graders in our mind's eye, from least likely known to most likely known:

- *inflammation*
- *sibling*

- *disease*
- *contagious*
- *prescription*

❊ What kind of vocabulary work should be done during reading?

Our preference is that clarification of words necessary for comprehension occur during reading, that is, at the point of use. For example, if a teacher is reading a story aloud, she can provide a word's meaning, parenthetically, right when the word is encountered (e.g., "The doctor tore off the prescription"—a prescription is a small piece of paper that a doctor writes his directions on—"[and] instructed Ramona to give it to her father . . . "). Notice that the explanation of the target word is simply folded into the text being read and the teacher quickly goes on with reading. Similarly, if the class or a group is reading together with the teacher, the teacher can intervene with a brief explanation. The reason for the "explain-quickly-and-go-on-reading" approach is what we have already noted: the primary goal when a text is being read—whether the teacher is reading or the students are reading—always has to be understanding the ideas being presented. Imagine a teacher elaborating *prescription*, by saying, for example, "Sometimes the doctor writes the name of a medicine he wants a patient to take. Sometimes he writes directions, such as drink plenty of water. Has a doctor ever written a prescription for you?" Such talk could take attention away from the ideas being presented in the story. The goal of explaining the meaning of a word during reading is to prevent the lack of knowledge of an unknown word from getting in the way of understanding the idea being communicated. If a teacher wants more elaboration of the words that were explained during reading (or for that matter before reading), that can be done after the story is completed.

There is, however, a problem with introducing words during reading: How can teachers introduce words during reading when their students are reading the story on their own? They can't do it as described above. That's one of the reasons preteaching plays a role. And that's one of the reasons why in the higher grades sometimes there are notes at the bottom of the students' texts with the definition of a word. (We must note, however, that too often those are traditional dictionary definitions that can be more difficult for the children than the word itself.) Moreover, it is not clear to us that the students most in need of clarification actually deal with those notes. In any event, it is the case that clarification at the point of use is not necessarily an option.

But clarification *near* the point of use can be an option if the teacher assigns students to read shorter sections of a text and then the teacher and the students discuss that section. At the point of assigning a section to be read, the teacher can do some quick preteaching (e.g., "You'll come across the word *inflammation* in the next section. *Inflammation* means that part of your body is sore and may hurt."). Such "near-the-point-of-use" clarification allows students to encounter the target word in close proximity to its use in context. So when it comes to words whose meanings are needed for comprehension of ideas, we would favor *during*-reading clarification, but if that is not feasible, then *before*-reading clarification. The words that were clarified may or may not be candidates for more elaborate after-reading instruction, which we take up below.

✳ What kinds of words get introduced after reading?

Beyond the words we've discussed above, the Ramona chapter is full of interesting Tier Two words—none of which is essential to understanding the story! Most of the words would add richness to the story, and all of the words would have long-term benefit for children's vocabulary development, so we would deal with them *after* reading the story. We will use four of such words—there are more—to discuss why the words are not necessary for comprehension of the plot of the story, and also why they are useful words to add to children's repertoires. For each of the words we start with the context in which they are found in the story.

- "[As Ramona sits in the lobby she thinks] about the *injustice* of having to wait to see the strange new Roberta." *Injustice* is a great Tier Two word to add to children's repertoires because it is a sophisticated and more complex label for the idea of something being unfair, and can be used across numerous domains: from the injustice of a court decision to the injustice of not getting one's turn. But it is not necessary for comprehension of the events in the story because before the sentence with *injustice* appears, there are several strong text statements that indicate that Ramona is annoyed and sad about not being able to see the new baby. Thus, when the *injustice* sentence is encountered, without knowledge of the meaning of *injustice,* most third graders will have already understood the important idea that Ramona is unhappy about not being able to see Roberta. So teaching *injustice* before the story is not necessary. However, because *injustice* is a great Tier Two word to add to children's repertoires, we would introduce it after reading.
- "The girls *longed* for their loving aunt, who was cheerful in times of trouble and who was always there when the family needed her." This sentence appears early in the story when Ramona and her sister are alone because Mr. Quimby has gone to the hospital with Mrs. Quimby. This sentence simply emphasizes the girls' loneliness, but it does not move the plot along. Yet longing for something is a sophisticated way of talking about wanting something and can be used in many contexts: longing for a friend or pet, longing for a resolution to a problem, longing for things to be different.
- "Ramona . . . saw her mother, holding a pink bundle, *emerge* from an elevator . . . " This sentence occurs toward the end of the story, when Ramona is waiting for her mother and the baby to leave the hospital, and she sees them come out of the elevator. *Emerge* is a sophisticated word that could be found in many contexts: beyond emerging from an elevator, a stem can emerge from a seed, a chicken can emerge from an egg, and an idea can emerge from one's mind. *Emerge* is a terrific word to add to children's repertoires.

- "Roberta is so tiny. Beezus was *radiant* with joy." When this sentence is encountered it has been well established that Ramona's sister, Beezus, is delighted with the baby. So that she is radiant with joy will generally be understood as something joyful and as such is not specifically needed for comprehension of the actual sentence, let alone the plot of the story. But knowing the meaning of *radiant* could deepen and enrich understandings of contexts in which it is used.

The words we just talked about don't come into play until after reading. However, in many cases there might be some words that were necessary for comprehension and thus introduced during or before reading that are also good additions to students' repertoires. These words would be taken up again after reading and given robust instruction. In this case, we decided not to follow up on the words we introduced before reading. Given the choices of words in this selection, the ones introduced before reading are more limited in use and more concrete in meaning. Thus we judge that they are both more readily learned from a brief introduction than the words we chose for robust instruction and not as broadly applicable.

> Ann Uzendoski, a first-grade teacher in Saint Paul Public Schools, sent us her favorite Tier Two vocabulary story: "Two first-grade students came running up to me and exclaimed excitedly, 'Mrs. U! Mrs.U! We have a *coincidence*! We have the same underwear!'" Mrs. U ended her message with "Needless to say, I did not ask how they found out!"

✳ What should I do about words whose pronunciation is difficult?

The short answer is tell the children (either before or during the story) that they will encounter several hard-to-pronounce words and then pronounce them. There are three such words in the Ramona story: *bassinette, stethoscope,* and *naugahyde.* It is likely that, once pronounced, *bassinette* and *stethoscope* will be familiar, but *naugahyde* won't. When the teacher pronounces the words, she can remind children that a *bassinette* is a baby bed, a *stethoscope* is what a doctor listens to your heart with, and then simply tell them that *naugahyde* is a kind of leather. There is no reason to make a big deal of such words.

HOW TO TEACH

At the outset of this chapter we noted that how to teach ranged from parenthetically explaining a word to robust instruction. One reason for different types of instruction is associated with *when* attention is brought to words. To reiterate, brief instruction is appropriate *before* reading, parenthetical explanation is appropriate *during* reading, and robust instruction is appropriate *after* reading. We covered some issues with parenthetical explanations before and during reading in the When to Teach section. Now we turn to our hallmark: robust instruction. We start with the assumption that the teacher has selected a set of words to teach—Tier Two words, with mileage (Chapter 2, pp. 8–9)—and that the class has finished reading a story in which the words appear.

✴ What are the steps for introducing a word using robust instruction?

Contextualize Words

New words should be introduced within a context. We find quite problematic a practice, seen more in high schools, of presenting students with a list of words that are simply viewed as good words for students to learn. Such a list has no context beyond being a list. In contrast, words that come from authentic contexts, such as the texts that students read or have read to them, provide a rich foundation for understanding new word meanings. The teacher can use the context in which the word was presented as the starting point for instruction. When a word comes from a text that students have read, the context has been experienced and can be used to advantage. Having read the story, students already have a set of connections they can link the word to. The following are two examples from the Ramona chapter of how introducing a word in its story context might proceed:

> In the story, when Ramona and her sister were home alone, they *longed* for their aunt, wishing she could be there with them.
> In the story, when Ramona first saw her new baby sister, she felt so happy that she was *radiant* with joy.

The importance of context in learning new words has been supported by very recent research with adults that shows that definitions on their own are not so helpful, but if they are presented with a context—or especially when they are preceded by a context—they become much more helpful (Bolger, Balass, Landen, & Perfetti, in press).

Provide Friendly Explanations

After presenting a word in context, the next step is to provide a general explanation of its meaning. In *Bringing Words to Life*, we provided extensive information about the inadequacy and complexity of typical dictionary definitions and recommended introducing word meanings by explaining them in everyday connected language, which we labeled "friendly explanations." Friendly explanations provide a complete sentence that includes the target word, in contrast to more fragment-like statements that are typical of dictionary definitions. We frame the explanations with words such as *someone, something, if,* and *you* in contrast to typical dictionary definitions that do not include agents who do, or use, or feel something. We think that using such words anchors the explanation and makes it more concrete. Our journey toward developing student-friendly explanations started early in our vocabulary research when we observed clearly how difficult it was for students to figure out the meanings of words from standard dictionaries. Below we attempt to underscore the distinction between traditional dictionary definitions and friendly explanations by providing examples of each for several words.

Word	Dictionary definition	Friendly explanation
devious	straying from the right course; not straightforward	If someone is devious, he is using tricky and secretive ways to do something dishonest.
vicarious	felt by sharing in others' experiences	If someone is getting a vicarious feeling, she is sharing an experience by watching or reading about it.
jaded	worn out; tired; weary	If someone is jaded, he has or has seen so much of something that he begins to dislike it.
exotic	foreign; strange; not native	Something that is exotic is unusual and interesting because it comes from another country far away.

The four dictionary definitions were among sets that were provided to students by researchers who then asked students to write sentences using target words. The following sentences that students were asked to write with the dictionary definitions available were fairly typical and provide evidence that dictionary definitions can be problematic.

He was devious on his bike. (McKeown, 1993)
We had a vicarious time at my friend's birthday party. (McKeown, 1993)
After the baseball game our team was really jaded. (McKeown, 1993)
The colonists were exotic in America. (Scott & Nagy, 1990)

Working to make definitions more comprehensible, we eventually came to the friendly explanation format. Little did we know at the time that some folks in England—the *Collins COBUILD Dictionary* developers—had developed a similar format. Thus, when we discovered the *COBUILD Dictionary* we were delighted, and to this day we use it as our first source for writing a friendly explanation. Sometimes we simply use the *COBUILD* explanation and sometimes we tinker with it, for example, to simplify the wording for target-aged students or to emphasize the sense of the words being taught.

Let us say a bit about other dictionaries—there are many. The table below presents the definitions from four dictionaries for the four words just discussed: *devious, vicarious, jaded,* and *exotic*.

Word	Source of definition			
	The American Heritage Dictionary of the English Language (Pickett et al., 2000)	*Word Central: Merriam–Webster Student's Electronic Dictionary* (2007)	*Longman Advanced American Dictionary* (Delacroix et al., 2007)	*Collins COBUILD Dictionary: English Language* (Sinclair et al., 1987)
devious	Not straightforward; shifty: *a devious character.*	sneaky, deceptive	using tricks or lies to get what you want	Someone who is devious is dishonest and secretive, often in a complicated way.
vicarious	Felt or undergone as if one were taking part in the experience or feelings of another: *read about mountain climbing and experienced vicarious thrills.*	sharing in someone else's experience through the use of the imagination	experienced by watching, hearing, or reading about someone else doing something, rather than by doing it yourself	Vicarious describes something that is experienced by watching, listening to, or reading about other people doing it or living through it yourself.
jaded	Worn out; wearied.	to make dull or uninterested by too much of something	not interested in or excited by life anymore, because you have experienced too many things: *New York musicians are jaded and tough.*	If you are jaded you have no enthusiasm because you are tired of something or because you have had too much of the same thing.
exotic	Intriguingly unusual or different; excitingly strange.	very different or unusual	unusual and exciting because of a connection with a foreign country: *exotic birds from New Guinea*	Something that is exotic is strange, unusual, and interesting because it comes from a distant country.

The online *American Heritage Dictionary* is a traditional dictionary, with traditional definitions. The online version of the *Merriam–Webster Student's Dictionary* is the electronic version of the publisher's intermediate dictionary, which is a specially edited (for 11–14-year-olds) version of the traditional Webster dictionary. The *Longman Dictionary* was originally designed for English language learners. It uses a core set of 2,000 words for all of its definitions. The *Collins COBUILD Dictionary* is similar to the *Longman Dictionary* in that it also was originally designed for English language learners. Each definition is in sentence form and starts with the target word and then explains the word.

The first two dictionary definitions use traditional definitions with perhaps the major difference being that the *American Heritage,* which is an adult dictionary, uses more sophisticated words in its definitions, while the *Merriam–Webster,* which is targeted to intermediate-grade students, tends to use more common words in its definitions. The major difference between the dictionaries in the last two columns is the format. The Longman generally uses more fragmented statements, while the *COBUILD* uses full sentences. We are very partial to using full sentences to explain a word because it provides students with a complete context and connected language that is easier to make sense of. The reason that most dictionaries use such cryptic language in their definitions is because of space limitations. That needn't be a concern with classroom instruction.

Provide an Additional Context for the Word

The other side of the usefulness-of-contexts coin is that care needs to be taken that learners don't limit their use of words to the contexts in which they were introduced. Thus, after the contextual introduction and word-meaning explanation, students should be presented with other contexts for the word.

For example, in the story *Bremen-town Musicians* (Plume, 1998), the word *exhausted* is used after some animals chased robbers away: "They felt so exhausted they had to rest." From this singular context, students might develop a tie between exhausted and being chased. So it would be important to introduce other examples such as being exhausted in the morning after staying up late or after baby-sitting all day for a younger cousin.

As another example, consider the use of the word *trepidation* in *The Wisdom of Goats* (Clough, 2005). In the story, an old goat feels trepidation as he walks to the village to tell the mayor that a storm is coming. The goat's trepidation stems from his anticipation that no one will believe him and he will be ridiculed. In order to forestall a limited association between *trepidation* and being scoffed at, other contexts that might produce trepidation, such as entering a house that is supposed to be haunted or giving a speech in front of the whole school, need to come into play.

Being able to generalize across contexts seems to characterize the vocabulary knowledge of higher ability learners. In a study with college students, Curtis (1987) demonstrated that low vocabulary students tended to define words in terms of a specific context—for example, in the case of *surveillance,* saying something like "that's what the police do"—whereas high vocabulary students were more likely to talk about surveillance in terms of "watching." The high vocabulary students' knowledge of words seemed to be decontextualized—that is, expressed in terms of general meaning. Thus, these students were more likely able to understand and use words across a range of contexts.

Provide Opportunities for Students to Actively Process Word Meanings

The theme that runs through the instructional activities that we recommend is that they encourage active processing in contrast to simply entering new information in memory. Rather than merely associate, for example, the word *inquire* with "to ask about something," we want students to think about the new information by combining it with known information. For example, why might someone *inquire* about what was being served for dinner? In the service of active processing, we ask students to consider uses of words, such as applying them to contexts or creating contexts for them. For example, students might be asked to decide whether *baffle* describes a situation in which a boy could not figure out a riddle, or to consider what a *hermit* might have a nightmare about.

A kindergarten teacher e-mailed us her reaction to her school's robust vocabulary program: "We love it!!!!" She then recalled an e-mail from one of her students' moms describing his reaction when he learned that she was having another baby (she also had a 15-month-old child at home). Her little kindergartner looked sad when he received the news, so Mom asked him how he was feeling. He said, "Discouraged."

A major goal of deep processing is prompting students to make connections between new words and words already known and situations that may apply to the word. So, for example, asking "What makes you feel *fatigued*?" invites students to connect fatigued with experiences in their own lives.

Another way to prompt students to make connections is to ask questions containing two target words that require them to figure out whether a connection could exist between the words. An important part of building the connection is to ask students to explain why they do or do not see a connection.

- Would you *berate* someone who had *inspired* you?
- Could *a tyrant* be a *miser*?
- Why might you *inquire* about a *dazzling* rocket?

The importance of deep processing derives from cognitive theory about how the human mind deals with information. According to this cognitive perspective, instruction that requires a learner to actively generate information helps the learner retain what's being learned because it helps build semantic network connections between new and prior information (Anderson & Reder, 1979; Craik & Tulving, 1975).

Given that generating information about new words is a good practice, you might wonder why the traditional task of asking students to generate a sentence about a word they've looked up in the dictionary yields such poor results. A typical performance, for example, might be "I saw a *philanthropist.*" The problem is that asking students to write a novel sentence may be requiring them to generate new information before they know enough about a word to do so. In a very recent study, generating sentences after reading a dictionary definition resulted in inconsistent performance, in contrast to asking students some open questions about target words (Nichols, 2007). For instance, consider some differences:

Student-generated sentences	Open questions and student responses
I am good at being *devious.*	What are some things someone might do that would be *devious?* • tell a lie
That was very *exploit.*	Why might someone want to have an *exploit?* • to be brave
It is very *inclement.*	What might it look like if it were *inclement?* • cold and stormy and wet

The vague and inadequate sentences in the first column certainly raise questions about what students can possibly be learning when asked to write sentences. Tasks that ask students to generate information about a word early in the learning sequence should provide some information that helps to scaffold the response. In the second column, the questions provide such scaffolding.

Provide for a High Frequency of Encounters Over Time

Beyond what we've described above for introducing words, robust instruction involves providing for lots more encounters with each word. The importance of encountering new words frequently is recommended by most vocabulary researchers and was well established by Mezynski's (1983) synthesis of eight studies and Stahl and Fairbanks's (1986) meta-analysis. In a very recent study with kindergartners and first graders (Beck & McKeown, 2007), students who received four times as many encounters produced twice as much learning.

Even though a number of encounters are important, the encounters should not simply be matching words with definitions or repetitions of the same context. The encounters need to include a variety of contexts and situations that encourage processing the words, as described in the last two steps above, and the encounters need to keep going over several days. For example, in our vocabulary studies in which comprehension was affected, the instruction was presented in a 5-day cycle for each set of target words (Beck et al., 1982, 1984).

Frequent encounters is a theme we have struck often because it is crucial to developing rich knowledge of words—knowledge that will be useful across contexts and will stay in memory. Experiencing lots of encounters with a word is a key to effective vocabulary learning not just because it helps you to remember the meaning, but because it helps you to bring a word's meaning to mind quickly when you meet the word in a new context. This is because those multiple encounters have created lots of connections to the word—each context in which you've experienced the word might create a new way to get to that word. Imagine you encounter the word *diplomatic* in a context about someone's less-than-frank response to a friend's new boyfriend. So the word *diplomatic* becomes connected to, for example, your accumulated knowledge of talk between friends, of friends' boyfriends, and of not being frank. That provides more pathways that lead to your understanding of the word *diplomatic* when you encounter it. The importance of that is in the fact that as we read, our mind needs to make split-second reactions to words and ideas if we are able to keep comprehension going. So if we can bring to mind an understanding of a word more readily, that helps keep comprehension going smoothly. If, as readers, we have to reach deep into our memories to understand a word too many times while reading, the train of thought breaks down. So we could even be reading something that contains no words that are completely unfamiliar, but still have vocabulary play a significant role in whether comprehension succeeds or not.

✳ What should I do with Tier One words that students don't know?

One possibility is that they do *not* need any attention. As mentioned in Chapter 2, we know that all students continue to add words to their repertoires during the school years, and it's most likely that this growth is in Tier One words—those are the ones students encounter on their own, either in informal oral contexts or in written materials that are targeted to young students.

But it could also be that some students will not add unfamiliar Tier One words to their vocabulary on their own because they simply won't encounter them. What may be needed, then, is simply making the words available. This could be accomplished by having more deliberate conversational interactions in the classroom. More conversation in the classroom allow students to *hear* more language—including a greater variety of words—and to *use* more language. Teachers can go about this by just being a bit more loquacious! Say things in more elaborated ways, play with language. For example, when visiting classrooms, you could well hear teachers tell students to "clear your desks." Imagine pausing and saying, "Hmmm, what does a clear desk look like? Is a clear desk like a clear sky?" Just let children think about this and respond—in a playful spirit. Notice this does not involve asking students "What does *clear* mean?" The point is not to elicit or provide a definition, but to make students aware of the *use* of the word and to encourage them to think about *contexts* in which it occurs.

The important points here are to put more language out there for students and to do so in ways that prompt interactions—get them to use language in response. Upping the language ante in the classroom requires few resources in terms of materials or classroom instructional time. Conversational interactions can be tucked into ongoing classroom events rather than requiring a piece of the classroom schedule. For example, as students are lining up, the teacher can playfully insert a number of position words that teachers have indicated can be tricky for young students, particularly English language learners (ELL) students: "Jose, please get in *between* Sam and Ben. Who is *behind* Clarence? Is Stacy *before* or *after* Maria? Who is in *front* of Serena? Hannah, please get in *front* of the line."

When trying to get students to look at you and be ready to work, a teacher could say something like, "I'm looking for a face that looks very excited . . . now I'm looking for a face that shows surprise . . . I'm counting smiles and frowns."

The importance of simple, informal conversation comes through in work that Hart and Risley (1999) did following their landmark study of children's vocabulary growth. The researchers found that children whose vocabulary continued to grow most productively were those whose families involved them in conversation about and beyond everyday events. Children whose families engage them in conversation expect to be talked to and expect others to respond to them. As they act in accordance with those expectations, they are able to enrich their own language environment, allowing them to learn more words and how to use them. Hart and Risley deliver what they describe as a "simple message" (p. xiii), which is that talking to children about things that are *not* important gives them experiences that *are* important to their cognitive development and future success. "Conversation matters," Hart and Risley assert, because it gives children the kind of practice that provides and sharpens their language tools.

We can do this for all children in school by creating the kind of classroom environment where talk is a regular part of the classroom format. The teacher talks to and listens to students, and students do the same with each other. This idea is captured nicely by Corson (1995), who suggests that "a rich language environment provided as part of the courtesy of good teaching" will go a long way to promote vocabulary growth for all students (p. 197).

The idea of taking advantage of conversation for students' vocabulary growth has been attended to more systematically by Barbara Wasik and her colleagues through what they call "conversation stations" (Bond & Wasik, 2007). In their professional development work with teachers, they request that teachers set up a specific area of the classroom for conversations or set aside a designated time for listening to children's conversations. These conversations can be between a teacher and a student who might have something he or she wants to share with the teacher. Or conversations can occur between children who want to share something at the "station."

Bond and Wasik suggest that when a child brings up a topic at an inconvenient time, the teacher should take care to let the child know she will be listened to at another time. For example, "Julia, we'd love to hear about how your sister did in the basketball game. Let's write that on our list of important things to talk about and you can tell us more at lunch or at the conversation station." To help teachers develop their awareness as conversationalists, Wasik and her colleagues offer questions for teachers to reflect on:

> Do you actively promote children's listening to and responding to what is being said in a conversation? Do you model it yourself? Do you give children time to finish their thoughts?
>
> Do you show respect for children's unique interests in what they'd like to talk about when they go "off topic" during a conversation? Do you gently steer them back to the topic? Do you make note of their interest and address it at another time that day?

✱ Can you give any guidance on teaching Tier Three words?

We can offer as guidance a number of distinctions that we think are important to keep in mind when considering Tier Three words. The first is that Tier Three words run the gamut from very concrete and imageable—for example, *mesa*—to very abstract and complex—for example, *culture.* A tricky thing about this gamut is that words on opposite ends of it may appear in the same lesson. We have seen lists of "vocabulary words" in content textbooks that contain, for example, both *mesa* and *culture, tundra* and *ethnic group, strip mining* and *energy.* Now these pairs of words may indeed be relevant to the same domain, but the problem is that they are often treated the same in instruction, that is, given the *same* kind and amount of attention when *different* attention is called for. For example, *mesa* is an easily explained and depicted physical formation. It can be described as "flat land with steep edges," and pointed out in a picture. It might be noted that it is the Spanish word for *table,* which could aid in envisioning the landform. *Culture,* on the other hand, is quite a broad and encompassing concept. It might be initially explained as "the ideas and customs shared by a social group," but to promote an understanding of the concept, teachers must offer examples of the kinds of ideas a culture might hold along with some discussion of what constitutes a "social group" that would have a culture. So is this a vocabulary issue?

Many Tier Three words that are of the more abstract variety are labels for major topics to be learned within content domains, and as such are not really what we think of as vocabulary. *Culture, nationalism,* and *revolution* are examples within social studies; *photosynthesis* and *mitosis* are two examples from science. Such words need to be taught within the context of the content domain that they represent. Definitions could be provided for such words—for example, *mitosis*: "the process in reproduction and growth by which a cell divides to form daughter cells." But comprehending that definition would by no means constitute an understanding of the process of mitosis. A student in biology would be expected to know how that process occurs: what stimulates it, what the results are, and its overall role in growth. So, again, is this a vocabulary issue?

It is important that instruction for words that represent content concepts explicitly explain how components of the concepts that the words represent relate to each other and fit within the domain (see Kucan, Trathen, & Straits, 2007, for further insights related to this idea). The notion of connection and explanation may be the tip of the iceberg of a larger issue with content teaching and learning. We often hear teachers say that their students have great trouble with content vocabulary. It seems to us that the problem may not be so much that the students are unable to understand the words and concepts, but that the concepts are presented in many content-area textbooks without adequate explanation and connection.

For example, consider an intermediate-grade science text unit on weather. The text draws students' attention to a graphic showing air molecules concentrated near the Earth's surface, directs students to compare the number of molecules near Earth with those higher in the atmosphere, and then asks "Why do you think there are more molecules near the Earth's surface?" A new paragraph then follows:

> Gravity causes a ball to fall to the Earth. Gravity also pulls the atmosphere to the Earth's surface. Gravity causes the gases to be pressed down on the Earth's surface.

The sentences on gravity seem intended to answer the question of why more molecules are close to Earth. But notice that explicit connections are missing. The first sentence on gravity talks about gravity's effect on a ball—and thus has no obvious connection to the previous discussion of the atmosphere. Although the next sentence talks about pulling the atmosphere, it uses terminology that differs from the question that it is supposed to answer. That is, the question talks about "more molecules near Earth," while the sentence in the gravity paragraph talks about "gases pressing down." We can imagine students reading this passage but being unable to explain what gravity is or what it has to do with air molecules being near the Earth's surface. We can further imagine a teacher thinking that students are having trouble with the text because of terms like *molecules, atmosphere,* and *gravity.*

For contrast, imagine how students might fare after reading the following explanation rather than the textbook:

> Why do you think there are more molecules near the Earth's surface? It has to do with gravity—that force that holds things near the Earth. You probably already know that when we drop things they fall down, not up, because of gravity. In the same way, the force of gravity pulls molecules of air toward the Earth. That is why there is a greater concentration of molecules in the part of the atmosphere closest to the Earth.

We think students reading this version would be better prepared to respond to questions about what gravity is and how it affects air molecules. They would not seem stymied by those terms. But is this a vocabulary issue?

Another concern around content words centers on the gap in words and experiences noted between children from different socioeconomic groups, such that many children seem to lack background knowledge of concepts attached to different domains. For example, primary-grades teachers told Blachowicz and Obrochta (2005) about students who were unfamiliar with such words as *athlete* and *circle*. In response, Blachowicz and Obrochta, along with the teachers, developed an engaging and feasible instructional approach that they called "Vocabulary Visits." The motivation for the format was that teachers remarked on how much information their young students picked up from going on school field trips. So they developed a format based on the kind of preparation and experience used in conjunction with field trips. The visits are each designed around a theme, such as weather, and begin with students responding to pictures associated with the theme and generating all the words they know related to the pictures and ideas they represent. A read-aloud on the theme is presented next, and work with the text elaborates understanding of the theme vocabulary. Writing activities are also included. Although Blachowicz and Obrochta label their approach "Vocabulary Visits," we would ask again, Is this a vocabulary issue? When do we separate vocabulary learning from the development of general concept knowledge?

✳ How might robust vocabulary instruction enhance students' writing?

We have found that there are several ways for teachers to encourage students to pay attention to words they use in their writing and to consider using the vocabulary words that they are learning. We suggest some direct approaches in the Menu of Instructional Activities (see Appendix A) such as completing sentence stems and describing a situation, person, or event that is related to a vocabulary word. We also suggest that students use their Vocabulary Logs (which we discuss in Chapter 4, p. 53) to record lists of words that they sort by categories, such as words that describe people or words that capture feelings. As part of prewriting or revising, students can refer to these lists to help them select interesting and precise word choices.

> One of Isabel Beck's graduate students reported that an instructional aide in a second-grade classroom took a child to the principal's office because he called her *boisterous,* a targeted word for robust instruction. We weren't sure whether she was unfamiliar with the meaning of the word—or knew very well what it meant and was not pleased by being so labeled!

A forthcoming book by Scott, Skobel, and Wells (2008) presents an approach to vocabulary that emphasizes writing through developing students' word consciousness. It begins with creating awareness and appreciation for the way authors select words for specific purposes and moves to helping students gain control over words they themselves use in writing. As students examine what Scott et al. call "mentor texts," students develop a bank of words. They are then encouraged to draw on this bank of words in their own writing.

The word bank for robust vocabulary that we talk about in (Chapter 4, p. 54) can be used in a couple of different ways to encourage students to be aware of how authors use words. One is to ask students to be on the lookout for uses of their target words, and when they find especially interesting ones to add those contexts to the word bank. Second, the bank could be expanded to include words that students notice in texts beyond the target words they are being taught. Getting students to notice words, as Scott et al. discuss, begins with the teacher modeling that process. So, for example, consider that our format for introducing words à la robust vocabulary always begins by drawing students' attention to the story context in which a vocabulary word is found. Having students read the exact sentence in which the word appears and talking about alternative word choices is one way to encourage them to begin to notice the impact of a carefully selected word. Asking students to consider how a particular word conveys a more precise image or feeling than another is an important analysis for students to undertake.

The process of noticing well-chosen words can move beyond target vocabulary so that students are alert to word use in what they read on their own or in other classroom reading. Consider that poetry can provide some compelling examples of word choice. Notice, for example, how, in the following familiar nursery rhyme, the word *nimble* captures perfectly one of the most important characteristics of a candle jumper: the ability to move with ease and lightness.

> Jack, be *nimble*!
> Jack, be quick!
> Jack, jump over the candlestick!

Wordsmith Emily Dickinson (1891/1997) provides dramatic contexts for her word choices, such as *abash* and *extremity* in the poem that follows:

> "Hope" is the thing with feathers
> That perches in the soul
> And sings the tune without the words
> And never stops at all,
>
> And sweetest in the gale is heard;
> And sore must be the storm
> That could abash the little bird
> That kept so many warm.
>
> I've heard it in the chillest land
> And on the strangest sea,
> Yet never, in extremity,
> It asked a crumb of me.

Abash robustly captures the idea of hope's resilience and its resistance to being destroyed. Chill lands and strange seas make the idea of an *extremity* come to life in the mind.

Students can find other examples of surprising or particularly apt word choices to bring in for sharing. Younger students can discover Jane O'Connor's books about Fancy Nancy (e.g., *Fancy Nancy and the Posh Puppy* [2000]). The stories focus on a little girl who is enamored of sophisticated words such as *ecstatic, spectacular,* and *unique.* Other picture books that focus on interesting words include *Max's Words* (Banks, 2006) and *The Boy Who Loved Words* (Schotter, 2006). Older students might explore the books by Lemony Snicket, such as *The Austere Academy* (2000), *The Ersatz Elevator* (2001a), *The Hostile Hospital* (2001b), and *The Vile Village* (2001c). Snicket shares his thinking about word meanings and his choice of particular words, which is exactly what we hope students will begin to do. Appendix B lists examples of many other books whose authors are well aware of the possibilities that words provide for shaping the images that their readers create. Some candidate Tier Two words from each book are also included in Appendix B.

Moving students to use more sophisticated choices of words in their own writing can be encouraged by asking students questions, such as the following, as they write or in conferencing with them about their writing:

- What words can you use to *show* your reader instead of *telling* your reader?
- What picture are you trying to create?
- What do you want your reader to know?
- What do you want your reader to think about all this? What words can you use to make the reader think that?

Specific attention to word use in writing—students' own as well as that of authors of texts read in class—is key to getting students to make better and more sophisticated choices of words as they write. Fundamental to enhancing word choice in student writing, however, is moving students to own the vocabulary introduced in class. That is, an ongoing robust vocabulary program, in which students are exploring word meanings and contexts, is much more likely to help students move what they are learning about words into their writing.

✳ What kind of assessment can you use to know that students are learning vocabulary?

First, let's clarify some issues of what people mean when they talk about "vocabulary assessment." It often means assessment of general vocabulary—what does a student's total store of words look like? The Peabody Picture Vocabulary Test (Dunn & Dunn, 1997) or standardized vocabulary subtests have this aim. Such tests provide a general idea of how knowledgeable a student is in vocabulary, especially relative to his or her peers. But these tests are blunt instruments that do not capture increasing knowledge of vocabulary words well at all. Consider that in aiming to test a person's general vocabulary, an assessment must select some number of individual words— the full vocabulary of a language is, of course, much too large to be captured on a test.

Thus, it is really an accumulation of knowledge of selected individual words that provides one's vocabulary score. Such tests might possibly reflect recent learning, if by chance some of the taught words appeared on the test, or if being involved in learning vocabulary allowed students to learn more words than were specifically taught—for example, through word consciousness or by being able to use their new learning to figure out additional words' meanings independently. But if students receiving vocabulary instruction do not reflect gains on standardized tests, it does not mean they have not learned what they were taught. Assessment of vocabulary *learning* means testing the *specific* words that have been introduced to students.

> We received the following e-mail from Tricia Fusco, an enthusiastic third-grade teacher from Pittsburgh, who immersed her students in rich vocabulary: "I made an open-ended test for the students and one of the questions was 'How did Ronald Morgan feel about going to camp at the beginning of the story?' Well, one of my *below-basic* students wrote a fantastic answer. He said that 'Ronald Morgan was *skeptical* about going to camp because he didn't think that he could win any medals.' I was so excited that I practically screamed it through the entire school!!!!!!!!!"

In considering how to design an assessment of vocabulary learning, the first issue is what is the purpose of the assessment? If you simply want to know if students can recognize the meaning of a word or indicate whether a target word fits a situation, you can use the traditional true/false and multiple-choice formats. (See examples in Chapter 6.) If you really want to know how well students have learned a word and if they can use it flexibly, then you will need to provide assessments that require them to go beyond recognition to generating meanings and situations for the words. First, let's consider two traditional formats and the variety of ways they can be used: true/false and multiple choice.

True/false items might be considered an old "work horse" in assessment. One issue to keep in mind is that true/false items can be developed to be relatively easy as well as rather hard. For example, consider the word *seniority* and the two items below:

- If someone has *seniority* it means they've been someplace longer than other people.
- *Senority* is related to time.

We see the second item as more difficult because it is more abstract, thus requiring a deeper understanding of the word.

For early primary-grades children, who do not know how to read yet, the teacher can present statements orally and children can answer on a response sheet by marking yes/no, or ☺☹. For example:

- If something is *usual* does it happen a lot?
- Does *drenched* mean very hungry?

Another issue that is important to keep in mind is that with true/false items there is a 50% chance a student can get an item correct through guessing.

In multiple-choice items, the guessing issue can be reduced to 25% by providing four choices, and, indeed, to 20% when an item provides five choices. Just as is the case with true/false items, multiple-choice items can be developed that are either pretty obvious or that require students to really think about the choices. Compare the two items for *diligent* below:

diligent

- fast
- hardworking
- lost
- punished

diligent

- making a lot of money
- working at an interesting job
- always trying your best
- remembering everything

Below is an example, using *clever,* of how four choices can be presented orally to younger primary-grades children who would not be able to keep four oral choices in memory. It's just a matter of developing a cluster of four yes/no items and asking each one separately. Notice that in the example below the first two items focus on a context in which the word might be used, while the third and fourth items focus on the meaning of the word. In presenting such an assessment to children, items should be mixed together with other items in a set so that all items for a particular word do not appear next to one another. Students can indicate their responses to each item by marking a response sheet as shown on page 36.

clever

- If you are a whiz at working puzzles, might someone say that you are clever?
- If you couldn't remember your phone number, might someone say that you are clever?
- Does clever mean trying hard?
- Does clever mean good at figuring out things?

Another multiple-choice format that reduces the chances of being correct by guessing is to include more than one correct response—sometimes two, sometimes three, and actually sometimes one. Using this format allows using only three choices rather than four. But by all means tell students that more than one response may be correct, as they are used to items with only one correct response! Thus, this format requires more thinking and extending students' thinking beyond a "one right" orientation. Below are examples of items that have one, two, and three correct choices respectively.

- If you met an *impudent* person, you would expect her or him to be:
  - rude
  - polite
  - safe
- If you were *conspiring,* you would need to:
  - have a weapon
  - meet with others
  - make a plan
- If you were an *eloquent* speaker, you would be able to:
  - pick the right words for any occasion
  - keep your audience's attention
  - earn your audience's admiration

For tests that are more challenging, pose questions that require students to develop examples, situations, and contexts for target words. In contrast to recognizing words' meanings and examples, which is what is required to respond to the formats above, the items below require students to use their language to construct responses.

- What might an *ally* do for you? Why might someone need an *ally*?
- What is something someone might do that would be *devious*? What might give you a clue that someone was being *devious*?
- Why might someone say a house is *typical*?
- What is something you might want to be *inspired* about?
- Tell about a time you tried to act *nonchalantly.*

In an environment of interactive rich vocabulary, the teacher is constantly exposed to students' thinking about words. Indeed, if instruction is rich and frequent, with lots of discussion, assessment is actually less important because you get such a good idea of how students are dealing with words during lessons. Assessment probably plays the role of confirming observations during lessons or providing an opportunity to get a read on individual students' knowledge separate from group discussion.

Our overall recommendation for developing assessments for a robust vocabulary program, provided in *Bringing Words to Life,* might be worth mentioning again here—that is, almost any of the formats we talk about for instruction can be used as assessments as well. (See Appendix A and Chapter 6.) Your choice of assessment should be guided by the student performance you are interested in getting a look at—What is it you want to see students do? On the flip side, you might also want to consider what it is you want students to expect. The kind of test provided might be interpreted by students as a signal of what is important to know or be able to do with the words they learn.

CHAPTER 4

* * * * * * *

Some Nitty-Gritties
of Instruction

In this chapter we cover some of the smaller details about what to do with words. These details represent a lot of issues and decisions that go into initiating and maintaining a vibrant vocabulary environment in the classroom!

* How should vocabulary instruction differ as you go up the grade levels?

The short answer to this question is "not that much"—that is, all the basic principles for effective, engaging instruction hold from kindergarten through high school. At all these levels, effective vocabulary instruction focuses on Tier Two words and provides explanations of their meaning, lots of contexts for them, and many opportunities for students to use and think about the words.

Of course, age-appropriate changes will occur, such as asking older students to apply more complex thinking to word interactions. For example, the kinds of interactions that require thinking about, say, three new words, and how they might relate would not be used with the youngest students.

Why might you feel *distress* in trying to *evade* an *appalling* animal?
How would you provide *reassurance* to someone feeling *vulnerable* from an *ordeal*?
Why might someone feel *reluctant* to help a *disheveled* person who seemed in *distress*?

With older students, more writing can be incorporated. Students might also be asked to work more independently. We recommend small groups early on. For example, students might be asked to respond in writing to the questions suggested

39

above—or groups of several students could collaborate on answers. But we would also include whole-group discussion time afterward where students read their responses and explain some of their thinking. Notice that the questions above cannot be answered with a "yes" or "no." It is important to keep the "why," "how," and "tell me more" going in vocabulary interactions because asking students to explain their reasoning supports active processing and making connections.

A school administrator e-mailed us: "We just love [the new vocabulary initiative]. Our kids are transferring it to all areas." The message also told us that a teacher had asked her students to give a "thumbs up" when they heard a vocabulary word in class. That led to the following story from some parents: Their son kept putting his thumb up during church. When asked why, the boy said, "The priest is using my vocabulary words."

Another way that vocabulary may differ somewhat as students move up the grade levels is that it may be more integrated with discussion of the texts being read. In the early grades, we always introduce words by presenting the context from the story, but that is often the only role that the story may play in the vocabulary instruction. As students mature, goals for their reading are more likely to include deeper consideration and interpretation of text ideas. So it makes sense to tie the vocabulary more deeply to the story.

For example, Edgar Allan Poe's classic short story *The Tell Tale Heart*, about an insane, paranoid narrator who murders an old man and then obsesses over a sound that he thinks is the dead old man's heart, is full of Tier Two words. Poe is known for having believed that every word mattered in telling a story. Below are some discussion starters for *The Tell Tale Heart* in which some of the interesting words in the story are linked back to important ideas in the story.

- The narrator tells us that he is not mad, that the disease had sharpened his senses, in particular, "the sense of hearing was *acute*." What happens in the story to support his point of view?
- In the story it was the "Evil Eye" that *vexed* the narrator. What happened that showed that the narrator was vexed?
- The narrator tells us he opened the door *stealthily*. Why was it necessary for him to open the door in such a manner?
- The story states that the police officers introduced themselves with perfect *suavity*. Where in the story did the narrator act with perfect suavity?
- What is the narrator referring to when he says the "*audacity* of my perfect triumph?" And why do you think he uses the word *audacity* to describe this triumph?
- The narrator said that he talked more quickly—more *vehemently*. How could his earlier description of the "overacuteness" of his senses cause him to interpret his talking as "more vehemently"?

- The narrator tells us that "he arose and argued about trifles, in a high key and with violent *gesticulations*." But it seems as if the police don't acknowledge his behavior. How could they ignore his wild gestures?
- The narrator reveals the buried body because he states, "Anything was more tolerable than this *derision*!" To what derision is he referring and why did it cause his confession?

✳ Should all Tier Two words get robust instruction?

As discussed in Chapter 2, even words within Tier Two don't all have the same mileage, that is, wide potential for applicability. Consequently, not all Tier Two words need robust instruction. Specifically, there are Tier Two words whose meanings are quite direct, for example, *dash* simply means "run fast." It is a Tier Two word because it is not the most basic way to communicate the concept and it more likely appears in written rather than in oral language. But it is readily learned, not only because its meaning is so close to a very familiar word, but because it is also very imageable. Such a word does not take a lot of instruction to be learned.

Our emphasis on robust instruction is based on two assumptions. First, vocabulary instruction needs to provide Tier Two words to students of all ages. And second, learning useful Tier Two words often requires robust instruction because those words tend to be more abstract and nuanced. For example, consider the word *meticulous*, which might be described as meaning *careful*. But *meticulous* is a very particular way of being careful—it is not the careful you need to be when crossing the street, but rather it marks a careful attention to getting the details right. So the short version is all Tier Two words don't need robust instruction, but many Tier Two words do need robust instruction.

✳ How many words should we teach at different grade levels?

There is no definitive answer to this question, but we can offer some guidelines. We have taught six words per week in kindergarten and first grade—and children have learned them at that rate. We taught groups of 10 words in fourth grade with success. So increasing to seven seems doable at second grade. Third graders can likely handle eight or nine words per week. At the upper grades—middle and high school—we feel comfortable recommending about 12 words per week. But we hesitate to go beyond that number, if the goal is to work with the words in a comprehensive manner and to encourage the students to learn the words deeply.

✳ What if a text has very few good candidate words that seem worth teaching?

Some texts are going to be much more word-rich than others—even texts that are at about the same grade levels. A strategy that we find very helpful when developing vocabulary instruction for a text is to use words *about* the text as well as words *from* the text. That is, there may be good interesting words that relate to the topic or some other aspect of a text even though they are not actually used within the text. Such words can be introduced by describing that feature of the text and then saying, "Another way to say that is . . . " and then introducing the new word, followed by a friendly explanation. For example, a fourth-grade class was reading the story *Night of the Pufflings* (McMillan, 1997), in which children help stranded baby birds to take flight. The teacher decided that the word *vigilant* fit the story, and introduced it in the following way:

> In the story, Halla paid careful attention to the puffins to make sure they were always safe. Another way to say that is Halla was *vigilant.*
>
> Someone who is *vigilant* pays close attention and concentrates on noticing any dangers or trouble there might be. Policemen are *vigilant* as they patrol the streets of the neighborhood.

Below are a few other examples from some popular stories:

> *Rosie: A Visiting Dog's Story* (Calmenson & Sutcliff, 1998): In the story, Rosie was trained to cheer people up who were sad, sick, or lonely. Another way to say that is Rosie showed *compassion* to the people she visited. When you show compassion, you try to help someone get through a tough time.
>
> *The Stories Julian Tells* (Cameron, 1989): In the story, Gloria really cared about Julian's feelings by not laughing at him when he fell over trying to do a cartwheel. Another way to say that is Gloria was *considerate.* To be *considerate* means to be thoughtful of the feelings of other people.
>
> *Yang the Third and Her Impossible Family* (Namioka, 1995): In the story, Mary was often ashamed and embarrassed by her mother's mistakes around others. Another way to say that is to say she was *mortified.* If someone is *mortified,* he or she may feel disgraced and want to hide from the embarrassing situation.
>
> *The Hot and Cold Summer* (Hurwitz, 1984): In the story, the boys were amazed to learn that Lucette was Bolivia's pet bird, not her baby sister. Another way to say that is the boys were *flabbergasted.* When you are *flabbergasted,* you are astonished and shocked by what you learn or see.

✳ When instruction is oral in the early grades, should you show them the written word?

We have always made the written form of the word available. In the early grades program we implemented for research purposes, we included each word on a card, which the teacher used when introducing the word to the class. We also recommended that the cards be posted all week while the words were being followed up. It seems a good idea to refer to the cards at times when mentioning the words. Indeed, we found that teachers did this naturally. But using the cards was seen as an opportunity to kind of familiarize students with the written form rather than explicitly to teach the students to read them.

✳ Should multiple meanings of a word be introduced at the same time?

Multiple meanings is the everyday term for *homographs,* which are words that are spelled the same, usually pronounced the same, but have different meanings. For example, consider *sound,* as in what we hear; *sound,* as in sturdy; and *sound,* as in the name for a body of water. These are different words, whose origins are from old English and various European languages and they are no more related to each other than, say, *volume, sturdy,* and *island.* We wouldn't see an advantage for teaching the latter three words together, so there is little reason to teach the first three words together. The point is that the three words have no common semantic features—the meanings are not at all related, they just happen to be spelled the same. So if they were taught together, there is a good chance of confusing students.

The notion of multiple *meanings* can get hazy because many words have multiple *senses,* and it can be hard to see the demarcation between multiple meanings and multiple senses. Multiple senses are related around a core meaning, that is, there is a common semantic origin. Various senses of a word emerge because language is flexible and ever changing as we use it. For instance, think of the word *mock,* which comes to us from the Middle English *moker,* via Old French *mocquer.* The original meaning is roughly "to mimic." Suppose the word appeared in a story and was used in the sense of making fun of someone in a mean way. In that case, we would likely not also introduce the sense of an imitation of something, such as a "mock" battle. Although both uses come from a common core meaning, they are far enough apart that it would seem unhelpful to introduce them together.

We see a somewhat grayer area with the word *model.* The central sense here is a representation of something. Consider *model* used in the sense of a model student— which, in essence, means the best possible representation, or ideal representation, of "student-ness." This sense is quite close to the use of *model* as a verb, as in "to model oneself after." The verb form usually connotes wanting to be like some excellent or ideal representation. Thus, we would likely introduce that sense and use *model* as a verb in the same instructional set—probably not the first day the word is introduced, but in follow-up activities on a subsequent day.

Would it also make sense to talk about *model* in the sense of miniature versions of something, often used as toys or collectibles? This use seems to move further away from the notion of ideal representation, yet the sense in which such a model represents something is rather readily understood. So this puts us right in the middle of the gray zone. The choice of whether to introduce this sense is up to personal judgment. We can imagine teachers who would think that talking about that sense would enrich students' understanding and use of the word, perhaps based on the knowledge that students have experience with these kinds of models. We can just as easily imagine a teacher deciding not to bring in another sense. The rationale in this case may include thinking that the "miniature model" sense is not that important and that students are likely to learn it on their own, or that it may be distracting to include the extra information.

A final point on multiple meanings is a case where it *is* a good idea to touch on multiple meanings. This occurs when you introduce a word that has a meaning that students already know. For example, if you introduce the word *fast* as "not eating," you would probably include that it also "has a meaning that we probably all know—if something moves very quickly, we call it *fast.*" Thus, even though the two meanings do not have a common core, the fact that the word form—pronunciation and spelling—is already attached to a familiar meaning suggests confusion is best avoided if the likeness is explicitly pointed out.

✳ What do you think about teaching students about morphemes?

There are distinctions, but not conflicts, between teaching robust vocabulary and teaching morphemes, which is the formal word for word parts: prefixes and suffixes (together known as affixes) and roots. Directly teaching morphemes usually aims to provide students with knowledge that will help them figure out the meanings of unknown words they encounter. Instruction for teaching morphemes is often associated with context clues, the motivation being that in the course of reading, when one encounters an unknown polymorphemic word, the reader makes a guess about the meaning of the word and uses the morphemes as a way of checking whether the unfamiliar word fits in the context (Nation, 2001, p. 264). So those are the differences. But the features are not in conflict because a goal of both types of instruction is to give students easier access to words they encounter—one directly and the other indirectly—toward enhancing student's developing literacy skills.

The issue of the role of morphology in promoting literacy growth is kind of a chicken–egg problem in that good readers seem to be aware of word parts and to use them to figure out meaning, and they seem to get better with this skill as they read more. So the situation can be likened to the general one of vocabulary: good readers tend to have good vocabularies, and those with large, flexible vocabulary repertoires tend to be avid readers. The question, then, is how to help students develop an awareness of word parts that actually can assist them in learning words.

Research on the effectiveness of explicitly teaching morphemic analysis tends to be iffy: some studies show it to be valuable, others do not. Students can end up learning what different prefixes or suffixes mean, but not necessarily being able to use this information to work out the meanings of new words (Curtis, 2006). In this way, the research mirrors the work on vocabulary instruction in general. Just as we can't simply provide information about word meanings and expect it to affect students' comprehension, we can't simply give students the meanings of word parts and expect them to be able to apply them to unknown words.

Despite the equivocal nature of the findings, most experts recommend some teaching of morphemic analysis (e.g., Baumann, Font, Edward, & Boland, 2005; Carlisle, 2007; Graves, 2006; Stahl & Nagy, 2006). Stahl and Nagy (2006) capture what likely motivates this recommendation in saying that "word parts are too valuable a resource to ignore." However, they go on to caution that "they are too inconsistent to use blindly. Students need to learn to use word parts strategically, cautiously, and thoughtfully" (p. 159). We fully endorse this recommendation and its cautions about the explicit teaching of morphemic analyses. The reasons for caution were well captured by Anu Garg (2007) on his A.Word.A.Day website:

> It's a phonic (and phony) world out there. We have megaphones and microphones. Megaphones magnify our voice, so why doesn't a microphone miniaturize it? We have phonograms but they are not the opposite of gramophones.

We would add an observation made by a 12-year-old we know: "Doctors don't doct and grocers don't groce." Or consider the high school senior who upon encountering the word *inept* asked, "Isn't that like when you give the job to someone in your family?" Well, your family member might be inept, but it actually turned out that he was thinking of the word *nepotism*.

On the other side of the morphemic blinking yellow light of caution reside words that are related, but whose relationship is opaque. Consider that *auction, authorize, inaugurate, augment, august,* and *auxiliary* all share the Indo-European root *aug-* (increase). But knowing the meaning of the root probably would not help a reader figure out the meaning of, say, *auction* if it was encountered in text as an unknown word.

Our general orientation to the issue of morphemes is to provide information on morphemes as part of developing students' understanding of their language and opening their eyes to the connections that language has. We want to give students a basis to understand how language came about so they can fit the pieces in as they find them. When students get information about word parts in the context of a rich vocabulary program, they seem to make lots of connections and begin to develop a sense of how language works. They notice patterns on their own—as fourth graders in our initial vocabulary study did when we taught the word *tyrant,* and they connected it with their knowledge of what a *tyrannosaurus* is like.

Being more specific, we can provide three recommendations: First, any direct teaching of affixes should be limited to only the most frequent prefixes and suffixes. The most frequent 20 prefixes and suffixes are found in numerous places (e.g., Stahl & Nagy, 2006; White, Sowell, & Yanagihara, 1989).

Second, we favor developing in students an awareness and appreciation for their language and its components by dealing with roots and etymology. Margaret McKeown talks about her experiences in this regard:

> "When I was teaching, I introduced my fourth- and fifth-grade students to the idea that the words of English actually come from several other languages. I

showed them examples from Anglo-Saxon, Latin, French, and Greek. They loved it! I showed them where they could find information about word origins in dictionary entries, and they went racing for the dictionaries. We filled the blackboard with examples from each of the languages as they called them out. They got so excited to see the "bones" of their language revealed as patterns within the languages began to show themselves. My motivation was to give them a window into their language—to forestall reacting to seeming inconsistencies in meaning and spelling by concluding that language is so goofy: 'Why is *cuff* spelled with two *f*'s and *cough* with a *gh*?' It makes language more transparent to understand that our language grew from contributions from other languages, and we can trace where words have come from and thus why we've ended up with what may at times seem like a hodgepodge. Although *homophones* have nothing to do with *homo sapiens,* knowing that the *homo* in *homophone* is from Greek, meaning 'same,' while the other is from Latin *homo,* meaning 'man,' can make language seem less baffling. Introducing students to historical aspects of language is done in the spirit of getting a grip on your language. Laying that foundation allows students a thrill of discovery when they notice, for example, that *company* shares a history with *companion.*"

Our third recommendation is to take opportunities to point out word relationships as part of follow-up interactions within robust instruction, that is, after a target word has been introduced and become familiar to students. We want to stress two important points here. One, it would not be done during initial robust instruction of a word. Two, we would not provide morphological information about every word or even most words. Rather, it would be done opportunistically as appropriate occasions present themselves. For example, *disruption* is a candidate for robust vocabulary instruction from the book *Frindle,* which we list in Appendix B. After students have encountered and worked with *disruption,* we might well develop a lesson to focus on the *rupt* Latin root. This could be an independent lesson or, even better, be implemented after another *rupt* word like *erupt* was encountered in something the students were reading. We could take the opportunity to focus on the *rupt* root, perhaps explaining that *rupt* means "break" and discussing how the notion of "break" fits in with

A Reading First director from West Virginia told us about her visit to a school building and a kindergartner who approached her and said, "You look *elegant.*" She thanked the child, but also wanted to know if indeed she understood the word, so she asked, "What do you mean by that?" To illustrate her intended meaning, the child drew back, and struck a pose as if ready to walk down a fashion show runway.

what they've learned about the target words *disruption* and *erupt* as well as with other words they might be familiar with, such as *interrupt, rupture, abrupt,* and *bankrupt.*

Finally, we emphasize that attention to morphemes is most valuable within the context of devoting ongoing rich attention to vocabulary development. Such a context provides opportunities for students to encounter many examples of relationships among words and to play around with how the different words fit into contexts and into language generally. Importantly, ongoing interactions provide encounters with morphemes through the words in which they are embedded. It is this accumulation of encounters that helps the morphemic patterns to become practiced enough that they become useful cues to meaning. That is, their meanings become readily accessible as students read and encounter the words and additional related words.

✳ Even if dictionary definitions are not very helpful, shouldn't students learn how to use a dictionary?

The dictionary is a resource that includes more information than definitions. All readers should know what information can be found in a dictionary and how to use it. Many people use dictionaries to check a spelling, a part of speech, or a syllable boundary.

When a dictionary is used to find a meaning, its value may be greatest when a word is kind of known and someone wants to check whether their understanding of the meaning is accurate. Of course, the dictionary is also used to find the meaning of a totally new word. It is in this domain that we have noted some problematic issues with dictionary definitions. And we have looked negatively on having students independently look up whole lists of words they have never encountered. There are, however, some ways to help students gain experience with using dictionary definitions to advantage.

To make deriving the meaning from dictionary definitions most effective, it needs to be modeled for students and practiced in a scaffolded way. A good way to begin might be for the teacher to work with some dictionary definitions, thinking aloud for students about how to use them to develop good explanations of word meanings. Here's what that might "sound" like. Consider the following context and dictionary definition for *adamant*:

> We took turns trying to convince Mrs. Gray not to give us homework
> over the weekend, but she was adamant.

> *adamant*: firmly fixed or decided, especially against something.

"OK, firmly fixed . . . against something. Well, it seems that Mrs. Gray was against canceling the homework—I guess that is how that part of the definition fits. So the 'against something' in the definition is not like leaning against something. Maybe it would be clearer to say 'against some idea or action' or 'against something that someone wants to convince you to do'? And 'firmly fixed' sounds like glued to the floor! I think it really means not wanting to change what you've decided—being firm about doing or not doing something. So let's start our explanation with: 'If you are adamant about something,' because we know from the sentence about Mrs. Gray that it is a way a person can be. Then add something about sticking with it; and then the opposition part—so, 'even if others are trying to convince you to.' If we put that all together we have: *adamant*: if you are adamant about something you stick with it and will not change your mind, even if others are trying to convince you to."

A few more examples of teacher modeling and then having students provide input would be valuable. Next, small groups could work in a collaborative way. Begin with a list of words from a story the class has read. Divide the class into groups and give each group several words—*and* the context in which they appeared. The task of each group is to develop an explanation for their words using the dictionary and the context. Their explanations need to be good enough so they can use them to teach the words to the rest of the class. Teacher input is important here! The teacher needs to monitor the groups and help them interpret dictionary language and make good decisions about how to structure their explanations. Also, this kind of exercise will be most effective if students are already involved with a vocabulary program and have experienced good explanations of word meaning.

✳ How do I fit in frequent encounters with words?

Encounters can be brief. Providing interactions with words should focus on letting students think about—process—word meanings and relationships. This does not require elaborate materials. In fact, oral questions and challenges are an excellent format by themselves.

It is not necessary to do *all* activities with *all* words. For a list of words you are working with, you might find that three or four fit together into some interesting format—for example, asking students if they ever tried to be *elusive*, felt *flustered*, or *flinched* at something. But if the same list contained *fugitive* and *meager*, such questions would not work. That's fine! For those words you might ask, What kind of television show might feature a *fugitive*? And how would you like a *meager* lunch?

A simple way to create encounters with words being worked on is to use them in conjunction with other contexts that arise in the classroom. For example, if social studies class is focusing on explorers, and a vocabulary word for the week is *deter*, you might ask what kinds of things may have deterred the explorers.

Another way we found to readily provide additional encounters is to take the target words from the story back into the story in which they appeared and challenge students to find other ways to use them in talking about the story.

We will use several Tier Two words (there are more) from *Doctor DeSoto*, the story of a mouse dentist by William Steig (1982), to illustrate how a teacher could take the students back through the story and ask them to use each word to describe a different aspect of the story. This activity would occur as part of vocabulary follow-up—that is, after the words are introduced, children have interacted with them, and teacher and children have discussed the words in contexts other than the story context.

- In the story, the fox thought about Dr. DeSoto as a tasty *morsel* to eat because to a fox a little mouse is a tiny bit to eat. Try to think of another way to use *morsel* to talk about the story. Here's a hint. Who else in the story might eat morsels of food? (In addition to Dr. and Mrs. DeSoto, moles and chipmunks are mentioned in the story.)
- In the story, the fox's mouth began to *quiver* when he thought about how good Dr. DeSoto would taste. Here (show picture of Dr. DeSoto looking in the fox's mouth) Dr. and Mrs. DeSoto are worried about what the fox might do to them. Who can use *quiver* to tell about what else is going on? (In addition to the fox's mouth quivering because he is afraid to have his tooth pulled, Dr. and Mrs. DeSoto were so worried about what the fox might do to them that they might quiver.)
- At the end of the story, the fox *stumbled* down the stairs with his teeth stuck together. Now (show picture of Dr. DeSoto on the ladder) think back to the part of the story when Dr. DeSoto was treating the fox's bad tooth. Ask children to use *stumbled* to tell what might have happened to Dr. DeSoto here. (Dr. DeSoto was so nervous working inside the fox's mouth he could have stumbled on the ladder.)

✳ Do you have any advice about how to handle a student's response to a word that is not quite on the mark?

It is important to help students build a strong representation of word meaning for the words they are learning. At times, this may include the need to redirect the uses the students develop so that they are always building on accurate information.

For example, consider the word *abundant,* introduced as follows: "If something is abundant, there is more than enough of it. There is plenty, and you won't run out." Imagine a student who is asked to think of something abundant coming up with the following sentence: "I had an abundant dinner."

It seems from this sentence that the student may indeed understand that *abundant* means lots of something, but the structure of the sentence makes it not quite an appropriate use. What you might do in this case is simply paraphrase the student's meaning, such as: "Oh, you mean there was a lot to eat at dinner, so the food was abundant?"

In other cases, students might be missing aspects of a word's meaning or use, and more information needs to be communicated. Margaret McKeown remembers sitting in on a kindergarten class in which the word *admire* was introduced as follows: "You can admire people or something that people have or do. That means you think that something about them is very special. For example, I admire people whose handwriting is neat and clear to read."

Asked to think of something or someone they admired, a student responded: "I admire gum." Now, it may be that the student thought gum was something special—

which is how the word's meaning was described, and which illustrates the limitation of definitions! In fact, this is a perfect example of why students need to meet words in many contexts in order to truly develop understanding of them. So, in this case, the teacher should provide some guidance about how the word is typically used. For example, the teacher might say: "Oh, I think you mean you really like gum—but *admire* usually means something we look up to and sort of want to be like. So, you might say that you admire the author who wrote your favorite book because you think that he is such a special writer."

✳ Is it helpful to use other modalities like having students draw or act out word meanings?

Using other modalities like drawing pictures or physically responding to words can promote connections to new word meanings. So, yes, this can be a good direction to take. A couple of notes here to assure getting the most for the money. A key to assuring that these activities are effective is using the "Why?" Ask, for example, why a drawing of brushing your teeth shows a *habit,* or why stomping around and growling shows being *furious.* Having students explain "why" confirms and reinforces the connections—between words and their characteristics, between new words and familiar related words. Also, make sure that the focus is on the word meaning and not on other aspects of drawing, moving around, and so on. And be careful not to spend too much time on an activity for a single word.

We have had success in having students put motions with some words that lend themselves to doing so. Below we present how we did this for inclusion in a research study (Beck et al., 1982) in which words had been grouped by semantic category—for example, "Working Together or Apart:" *foe, compromise, ally, conspire.* The words in one of the categories, "How We Can Move Our Legs," lent themselves to pantomime. So after the students had had the words introduced and had some experience interacting with them, the teacher explained that she was going to read a story and that each time she came to one of the words in the "legs" category they were to move their legs that way. Since the activity was designed to reinforce the meanings of the words, it was important that the movements the students did in response to the story corresponded to the meanings of the words. To ensure this, we offered corresponding movements. And it was suggested that students practice them before applying them when the teacher read the story.

- *stalk*: Tiptoe cautiously, making frequent stops, peering about as you move.
- *galumph*: Stomp your feet as you walk, moving slowly and heavily.
- *vault*: Pantomime jumping over an object, putting your hands on it as you take a leaping step.
- *trudge*: Walk slowly, dragging your feet, with slumped posture.
- *patrol*: Pace back and forth a few steps, walking crisply and looking closely at things as if guarding them.

- *meander*: Take a few slow, casual steps in no particular direction with hands in pockets or clasped behind back.
- *strut*: Walk with accentuated upright posture, head up, taking quick steps.
- *lurch*: Stand, then make a sudden jerking movement, letting the knees bend and heaving forward.
- *dash*: Take a few short running steps.

Below is the "moving story" that the teacher read.

Jackie wanted an adventure so she decided to go out *stalking* wildlife. As she left her house, Mr. Paine's dog *dashed* after her. He wanted an adventure too. When Jackie and the dog got close to the forest they noticed a big horse *strutting* around a pasture. "What a handsome stallion," thought Jackie, "and how proudly he walks."

They entered the cool, dark forest. Before Jackie's eyes got used to the darkness, she nearly tripped over a turtle *trudging* along the path.

Suddenly she heard footsteps thundering behind them. She jumped out of the way just in time, as a gorilla *galumphed* by. "Wow, *stalking* wildlife can be dangerous!," she said.

She walked quietly behind the gorilla until they came to a clearing. There Jackie stopped to watch a moose as he *meandered* about the open area.

Jackie happened to glance up and see a panther walking back and forth in front of a cave on the hillside. "She must be *patrolling* her den where her cubs are," Jackie thought.

Jackie was enjoying watching the wildlife and not being seen. Next she looked way up on the hillside and saw a lion sunning himself on a rock. As she watched, the lion rose up on his hind legs and began waving his paws in the air. Suddenly, he *lurched* forward, lost his balance, and fell to the ground below. He let out a loud bellowing cry as he lay on the ground.

"He must be hurt," thought Jackie. She ran to the edge of the forest where Dr. Rogers, the vet, lived. Jackie knocked on her gate. When Dr. Rogers opened the door Jackie told her about the lion. Dr. Rogers called, "I'll be right there!" She grabbed her bag, ran out of her house, *vaulted* over the fence, and rushed into the forest.

Jackie decided she'd had enough wildlife for one day. She started home and Mr. Paine's dog was right behind her.

As they approached Mr. Paine's house, Mr. Paine appeared and called out, "Hello! Have you two been for a walk?"

"Not exactly" said Jackie. "Your *dashing* dog and I were *stalking* wildlife. We saw a *strutting* stallion, a *trudging* turtle, a *galumphing* gorilla, a *meandering* moose, a *patrolling* panther, a *lurching* lion, and a *vaulting* vet!"

The teacher reported that the students loved doing the activity, especially the last paragraph, which they wanted to do again and again. By the way, to reduce the potential for "too much activity" we suggested that students be told that they could move no more than three steps from their starting point during this activity.

Of course the "legs" words readily lent themselves to pantomiming, but other words can be pantomimed too. Below is an example a teacher provided to us, using the following words and motions:

- *clever*: Touch your head, like you're a good thinker.
- *frugal*: Act like you're counting your money, because you want to keep it and not spend it (hand motion of counting out bills).
- *appreciate*: Bring your hands together and bow your head slightly to show being thankful.
- *splendid*: Spread your arms wide, to show something wonderful!

Below is the story the teacher read, which she called *A Boy and His Money*.

Once there was a *clever* boy who did not *appreciate* the value of money. He loved to spend it. His mother was always telling him to be *frugal* with his money, and not to waste it on things like toys that broke easily and candy every day. But he thought things like that were just *splendid*!

So he kept up his wasteful ways until one day his mother forgot to give him his lunch money. He did not have any money of his own because he had spent it all on candy the day before. Oh, was he hungry! He did not feel so *clever* then. He was lucky though. His teacher loaned him the money. He *appreciated* that a lot! And from then on he was much more *frugal*. He told his mother about his *splendid* teacher when he got home, and how he had learned to *appreciate* the idea of being *frugal*. "Ah, you are a *clever* boy after all!," his mother said.

A word of caution: be careful not to try to put motions with too many words. Not all words lend themselves to motions, and too much of a good thing can be a problem. It's best to put a motion with a word only if you can kind of "see" what the motion might be like.

Finally, incorporating movements doesn't have to involve a story. Children enjoy doing motions (e.g., *astonished, cower, perplexed*) and you could just demonstrate a motion and have children imitate you.

✳ Should we post vocabulary words on the wall?

We think that the words in play—those introduced and currently being practiced—should be publicly displayed. And it may be useful to keep that list up through the next week, adding the subsequent list of words to the display. But we would not leave all the words up indefinitely—at some point it gets to be just word wallpaper! The point of having words on the wall should be to *use* them, to keep them active. So the posted words should be a focal point for thinking about and noticing how they are used, or when they come up in other contexts and for reminding students about words they might use in discussion or writing.

✳ Should students keep a record of some kind with their words in it?

Yes!! Students should have their own record of the words they are learning. The one we use is what we've called a "Vocabulary Log." We first used it in our research studies with fourth-grade students and found that it seemed to play an important role in the classroom and for the individual students. In fact, we know of one student, Dana, who kept her log throughout her schooling and into her own teaching career! We came to learn this because Dana's mother was a teacher and then a principal in the district where we conducted our first vocabulary study. Some years later when we were working on entirely other research in the district and ran into Dana's mom, she told us about her daughter's log a couple of times. Once, when Dana was in junior high, Mom told us that she still used it as a reference for the words she'd learned. Many years later, when we visited the district and talked to Dana's mother in her capacity as principal, she told us that Dana had become a teacher—and still had her log!

The log we used in our studies was simply sheets of paper, three-hole punched, in a small notebook. Completed log pages contained each word, its friendly explanation, and a good sentence using the word. These are the essential parts of a record for students: the word, an explanation of its meaning, and a good context sentence. How those come to exist on the page, and the kind of format the log takes are flexible.

Some teachers have suggested individual index cards for each word. This format lends itself to easy word sorting, selecting individual words to use in activities, writing, and so on. But keeping track of all those index cards could create a bit of a headache! So using sheets of paper in a notebook is a good alternative.

For our logs, students had to fill in some part of the information each time, but we also gave them some support by supplying information. For example, we always had the words already on the page. The explanation was sometimes there or sometimes partly there to be completed, as was the sentence. Sometimes students had to write all of the explanation or sentence.

We sometimes had the class develop the explanation and sentence together and all wrote the same one on the log page. At other times we had students develop their own, often in pairs or groups. But there was always an opportunity to share and discuss the explanations and sentences—and most important, the teacher always checked to see that good explanations and meaningful contexts were used. This assured that students would have a good resource to use if they wanted to check on a word's meaning or use.

> This note was passed along to us from a teacher in Beavertown, Oregon: "One of my lucky students got to travel to California to watch the baseball game. On the flight back, his dad was working on a crossword puzzle and needed a six-letter word for friendly. My student, Grant, said, "I know! *Genial!*" And he was right! *Genial* was one of our recent vocabulary words. I'm sure his dad was impressed with that one!!"

In deciding how much support to give students in filling in their logs, teachers need to consider the extent of support students might need and how much effort the teacher can realistically devote to preparing the logs. Students at fourth-grade level or above might be expected to complete all of the information in their logs over the cycle of lessons on their own. Younger students may require some support. For students as young as kindergarten and first grade, just a classroom record of the words may be sufficient. In fact, it is probably not worth the effort it would take students this young to record such information on their own. The time could be better spent on oral practice and use of the words. A classroom record can serve as a resource for individual students or for the teacher's use in reminding or prompting uses of the words.

✴ What should happen to words after they have been taught and worked with for a week?

In trying to provide multiple encounters in instruction, it is helpful to think about encounters over time and place—what we think of as "widening circles of vocabulary engagement." That is, although it is important to provide multiple encounters in the initial sequence of instruction, you can increase the possibility of the words being learned well by giving attention to them beyond that. Here we talk about how to keep attention to words beyond the sequence in which they are taught, beyond the classroom, and beyond school.

First of all, keep them around. There should be some resource in the classroom where all words that have been taught are kept and are accessible to students and teacher. We think the most useful format is a "word bank"; that means different things to different people, so let us describe our idea. Write each new word on the top of a large index card. Write the meaning and a context—this can be the original story context or some context that came up in class and was popular. As each set of words is introduced, file the past set in an accordion folder, alphabetically. A file of separate index cards provides the most flexible resource for words. Kept that way, they can be arranged and rearranged, sorted, and pulled out one or several at a time. These words, then, remain available for quick tasks, and for checking with in the case of future encounters.

This word bank resource might be used in some quick ways when a few spare minutes are available, perhaps between activities or at the very beginning of the day:

• Ask a student to pull three words from the word bank for the class to use in a quick write: "Your words are *fugitive, diplomatic,* and *scarce.* Take a few minutes and see if you can write a paragraph that uses all three."

• Grab a word and quiz the class on its meaning and challenge them to create a sentence: "Here's a word we had a few weeks back: *mundane.* Who can tell us what it means or use it in a good sentence?"

• Pass out a few words to groups of students and ask them to think of a way they could have used the word over the past few days: "Your word is *scarce*. What have you thought about or read about or done in the last few days that had anything to do with things being *scarce*? Think of how you could have used that word, or maybe how an author you were reading could have used it."

Another way to keep words active or to bring them around again is to use previously taught words in conjunction with a text being read currently. This can occur in several ways. The teacher might go through the words and deliberately choose relevant ones to connect, or the teacher might present a word or two and challenge students to think of how they might apply it or them to what is being read. For instance, let's say that your words for last week included *distraught, sympathetic,* and *avoid*. And your class is now reading the Ramona Quimby story discussed earlier, in which Ramona gets a new baby sister, but experiences some difficulty in trying to visit her mother in the hospital. After the class reads the story, you might pose the following questions in discussion:

> Do you think Ramona felt *distraught* when she was told she had to wait in the lobby?
> Who in the story seemed *sympathetic*?
> Do you think not allowing younger children as hospital visitors is a good way to *avoid* spreading germs?

Another way to do this might be to suggest the three words, *distraught, sympathetic,* and *avoid,* and ask students if they see any way they might apply to the Ramona story.

✳ How can I extend vocabulary use into the school beyond my classroom?

Involve other teachers. Give the art teacher, the gym teacher, and the crossing guard lists of words students are learning and see if you can entice them into using the words in the presence of the students. You may not find that all teachers and staff want to play along, but it is our hunch that in every school you can find a few who will delight in it! We have heard about vocabulary-active crossing guards, school secretaries, and custodians! A way to get other school staff—or any visitors to the classroom—involved in vocabulary is to post words on the classroom door. This can be the current list of words or ones that you'd like to have reviewed. Visitors are then alerted to which words students are learning, and they can participate. For example, the librarian might drop by and, seeing the list of words, mention that she has a book to recommend that is *appropriate* to the season.

Some kindergarten teachers at Clayton Elementary School in Pittsburgh involved other grade levels in vocabulary by having their students visit the upper-grade classrooms for a "quiz." The kindergartners went into fourth- or fifth-grade classrooms with a handful of their vocabulary words on cards. An upperclass student picked one of the cards, and the kindergartner either explained the word or used it in a sentence. If they could do so correctly, they got their picture taken in a delightful wizard costume that one of the teachers had designed.

An engaging way of having students take their vocabulary learning schoolwide was described to us by Kathy Brita, a very talented teacher in Fort Wayne, Indiana. Kathy wrote:

> "I am buying from Office Depot those plastic name tags that hang from a shoe-string necklace. We're going to put a selected Tier Two vocabulary word in each one. The kids will wear them and all the staff will enter into the fun. When they see a child wearing one, they will talk with the child and use the word in context. The children will report back to the group the many ways that the word was used by staff members or even other students."

Take words out of the classroom and into the hall by making a public bulletin board a center of vocabulary attention. Using public-area bulletin boards for vocabulary displays might get multiple classes or grades involved in vocabulary and might even set off a little competitive word use. Start with some questions that contain a vocabulary word from, for example, each grade's current list:

> Are fourth graders *diligent*?
> Do fifth graders think homework is *oppressive*?
> Can sixth graders do *extraordinary* work?

Challenge students to respond to any of the questions with answers that contain a vocabulary word. Such responses might include:

> "Fourth graders are so diligent that they always *satisfy* their teachers."
> "Sixth graders do extraordinary work because they are *studious*."
> "No—fifth graders think homework is an *injustice*."

Another competitive bulletin board activity might involve putting up a word from each grade, posted along with student work to exemplify the word's use. At the end of the week, there could be a vote for the best word uses. Another approach is to post an interesting picture and have students write sentences to describe the picture using their vocabulary words. Pictures can be selected from those crazy shots that people send around to friends on the Internet—you know, dogs cooking, cats riding donkeys, and the like. A "sentence of the week" might then be selected.

✱ There are lots of ways that students can be encouraged to use words outside of school. What are your favorites?

Of course our favorite is the Word Wizard activity we described in *Bringing Words to Life.* This remains our favorite probably because it got such a strong response from students—which was a stunning and exciting surprise for us! We thought it might be a kind of cute activity that got some students engaged in looking for words outside of class. But it turned out to be much more than that, with nearly every student bringing in word sightings and word uses daily! Just to remind readers how this worked, we had the teacher offer points when students could describe having heard, seen, or used one of their vocabulary words outside of class. Points were tallied on a chart that had each student's name across the bottom. Periodically, the teacher tallied the points and awarded certificates and "prizes" such as extra center time or reprieves from a homework assignment.

There are lots of possible variations on the theme of getting students to keep alert for their words or ways to use them outside of school. And it seems to work at all levels, even in high school! We know this because a friend told us about walking past his high school son's room one evening and hearing a brief whoop of excitement. He walked in and asked what was up. His son happily told him that he had found two of his vocabulary words in the chapter of the book he was reading. It turned out that his English teacher simply asked students to report it if they found any of their vocabulary words in their reading. For this student, at least, just the finding of words was engaging enough, without any need for earning points or other rewards.

But if incentives are needed for students that are too old for Word Wizardry, one you might try is a "vocabulary credit card." Finding words can earn them credit, which they log into an account. They can then "spend" their credit by using it against, for example, homework assignments, or quizzes.

A rather straightforward way to get students to take their vocabulary learning out of school is to assign specific homework related to their words, such as finding one of their words on a television program or in a book they read or on an Internet site. Here's a variation on assignments asking them to find their vocabulary words that may challenge the students a bit more: rather than finding a word, ask them to find a context in which one of their vocabulary words could have been used, but wasn't—for example, a situation in a television program that fits the word *compatible*.

Especially if some students are reluctant to take on the challenge of finding word use outside of school, it helps to tailor the assignments as much as possible. That is, direct the requests to find or use words to activities that you know students are engaged in, such as soccer, video games, or whatever. If you ask students to think of words that might be used during a soccer game, or to describe how they feel when playing soccer, they may well find relevant vocabulary words coming to mind even if they aren't deliberately trying to think of them!

Finally, remember that it helps the enterprise tremendously if you share your own word finding with your students. If you happen to see vocabulary words used in the newspaper or in what you are reading students will enjoy learning about it. This also helps them understand that these words they are learning are not just part of a classroom exercise, but have real life beyond the classroom.

We've had a number of reports of students' delight in experiencing vocabulary they are learning in real language. For instance, Darleen Operanozie, a teacher in

Pittsburgh, told us about her third-grade son who upon hearing the word *flabber-gasted* used on television literally rolled off the couch. "That's one of our words!," he yelped to his grandmother. Grandma played as if she didn't know the word, and he happily explained it to her, with a full complement of facial expressions: "If you're flabbergasted, you're just, like 'Wow! Oh my gosh! For real??!!' It's something that is really, really a surprise!"

CHAPTER 5

* * * * * * *

What about English Language Learners?

W e've had teachers ask us about a number of issues related to vocabulary instruction and students for whom English is a second language. The issues have crystallized into the two questions we respond to below.

* Is instruction in Tier Two words appropriate for English language learners?

To respond to the question of Tier Two words and English language learners (ELLs), we begin by first underscoring the critical nature of vocabulary knowledge in understanding language through relaying an experience that Isabel Beck had as a second language learner—a German language learner (GLL). We will then discuss the role of robust instruction for ELL. Isabel writes:

"Many years ago, I went to Germany with my husband, a political scientist, who had gotten a grant to do research at Radio Free Europe in Munich. With my husband's less than mediocre German, and the many Germans who spoke at least some English, we managed to get ourselves situated in a small apartment in a residential neighborhood. In the year that I lived in Munich, I went from being a non-German speaker to being a fairly adequate speaker in everyday conversation. I could shop, talk about the weather, ask neighbors about their families, get directions for taking the bus, explain what I was doing in Germany, and the like. Toward the end of my year in Germany, I became friends with two women who lived in the neighborhood and was invited for coffee (and exquisite pastries) with them several times.

"One of my friends, Maria, was a middle school math teacher; the other,

Elice, was a photographer. Elice once tried to turn the conversation to current political issues in Europe and the United States, but I was at a loss to engage. At another time, Maria attempted to turn our conversations from small talk to differences in schooling and teaching in Germany and America, but I was not able to understand much of what she said. Moreover, when Elice, who spoke English fluently, translated Maria's questions about teaching in America, I was unable to answer them in German. And there it was, I had hit the *lexical bar*!

"The lexical bar, which we mentioned in Chapter 2, is a concept developed by Corson (1985, 1995) to characterize the distinctions between everyday oral language and academic, literate language. Compared to oral language, literate language has a greater variety of words and a greater density of high-content words, and the words are less concrete and longer. I had become quite familiar with everyday German vocabulary, but not with academic, literate vocabulary. The latter is not common to oral conversation; rather, these are the words that are found in written language.

"As an example of the distinction between everyday vocabulary and literate vocabulary, I developed the table below to provide a sense of the kind of German words that I had learned from conversation in contrast to words I would not have known at the time Maria, Elice, and I chatted. Let me explain further by talking about the words in each column of the table.

"In the first column, I listed some words that I knew in German. I avoided obvious nouns, especially those that people can see around them, such as *sky, store, house, river, children, women, church, streetcar,* and the like. It was a long time ago, but I was able to spark my memory by thinking about situations during my life in Germany, and picturing people and places. For instance:

- "I often told folks that 'I was *confused* about how to . . . '
- "I asked a German-English speaker what the word for *slowly* was as I often wanted to ask folks to speak slowly.
- "I can remember distinctly asking an elderly gentleman about where I could find a parking place. I remember the man well because after I asked my question, he furrowed his brow for moment as if saying, 'I don't quite understand what you're asking,' and then a moment of clarity appeared on his face, and he repeated in precise German, 'Oh! Where can I find a parking place?' He replied in clear and slowly uttered German with gestures 'around the corner and behind the church.'
- "My memory for learning *other* had to do with seeing people pointing to things behind glass in bakery shops and saying, '*the other*' or '*a different one.*'
- "The word *worried* came to my consciousness when a German acquaintance told me that he was worried about being able to go skiing over the weekend because the weather would likely be poor.

"Of course, there are, perhaps, several thousand words for which I have no memory of how I learned them, but I do know that I didn't study German and my husband and I did not speak it in our home—rather, I learned it from engaging in everyday life. It took me about a year to be moderately adequate in conversational German, which is in concert with Cummins's (1994) notion that it takes ELLs about a year or two—obviously on average with large individual differences—to manage everyday English conversation. I was not, however, able to manage academic, literate German as indicated by my inability to converse with Maria and Elice about current events or teaching as I would have with a fellow American teacher.

Everyday words I knew in German	Words in newspapers	Words in academic reading material
confused	feud	parenthetically
slowly	intensified	elaboration
parking	administration	clarification
corner	officials	enhancement
behind	voluntarily	encounter
different	require	tolerate
other	classified	repertoires
worried	forced	contextualized

"Toward capturing the problem, in the second column of the table, I listed eight words from about 50 words (not including proper names) of a front-page newspaper article from an American city for which I would not have known an equivalent German word. In the third column, I listed some of the words from the first page of the Introduction of this book for which I would not have known the German equivalent. So, if the newspaper and the book were in German, my lack of academic, literate German vocabulary would limit my access to them. (Notice that the words in the second and third column of the table are Tier Two words, while the words in the first column are Tier One.)"

Much of the problem for ELLs lies in the distinction between words in the first column and those in the other two columns. In contrast to the year or two that it takes to learn the kinds of words in the first column and thus be able to manage conversation, Cummins's work suggests that it takes 5 to 7 years to cross the lexical bar to the meaning system created by academic, literate culture. This makes contact with the findings of Hayes and Ahrens (1988) on the sharp distinctions between the wordstock of informal oral language and that of written language. All students, including ELLs, need to cross the lexical bar to achieve any measure of academic success. It is our position that all students need to start crossing early. The question that then arises is, What is *early*?

For us, *early* means that when ELL students can manage everyday conversation—perhaps to the extent that Isabel Beck could in German—students should receive instruction in Tier Two words. And given that the words being considered are Tier Two words, the assumption is that native-speaking students will not know those words either. Thus, instruction for ELL students can be done along with their native-speaking classmates. To take a deeper look at what we are suggesting, we first ask you to answer the questions below.

1. Is it likely that native English-speaking 5-year-olds know the meanings of the following words *in English?*
   table
   mother
   beautiful
   sleep
   run

2. Is it likely that native Spanish-speaking[1] 5-year-olds know the meanings of the following words *in Spanish?*
   table
   mother
   beautiful
   sleep
   run

3. Is it likely that English-speaking 5-year-olds know the meanings of the following words in English?
   astonished
   cherished
   devotion
   reluctant
   triumphant

4. Is it likely that Spanish-speaking 5-year-olds know the meanings of the following words in Spanish?
   astonished
   cherished
   devotion
   reluctant
   triumphant

---

[1]We use Spanish speakers as an example of second language learners, but are fully aware that there are many, many other languages represented in schools. In fact, Kindler (2002) noted that "more than 460 languages were reported to be spoken by limited-English-proficient (LEP) students in the United States" (cited in August & Shanahan, 2006).

We assume that your answer to item 1 is Yes. Thus there is no need to teach English-speaking children the meanings of those words. We also assume that your answer to item 2 is Yes, so there is no reason to teach Spanish-speaking children the concepts underlying those words. The instructional issue is that Spanish-speaking children need to learn the English labels for words they know in Spanish. For example, if they didn't know the English versions of the words in item 2. If they understand what the words mean in Spanish, they will understand what the words mean in English when they learn the English labels. And many of those labels will be learned through everyday encounters because they are used frequently in conversation and are highly concrete.

Certainly, native speakers have larger Tier One vocabularies than Isabel Beck had in German, or than ELLs who have been here about 2 years have in English. But with enough second language understanding to "get along on the street," we see little reason not to start introducing children to Tier Two words with one proviso, which is the same for both native and second-language speakers: that the underlying concept is understood. That is, for example, if children know what *angry* means either in English or Spanish, they can be taught what *livid* means. Of course, larger Tier One vocabularies will allow more enhanced conversation about everything, including the meanings of words, but we are offering a minimum requirement for starting the move toward the lexical bar.

Nevertheless, a question remains of how much instructional time should be given to Tier One words. Certainly some is needed. But Tier One words will continue to be acquired from everyday life, including everyday school life, so there is a need to conserve classroom time on what is *not* so hard to acquire and likely available from oral informal language: Tier One words. In contrast, the majority of direct instructional time should be targeted to Tier Two words, which are more difficult to learn and less likely to be available from oral conversations.

In summary, about the need for Tier Two words, it is essential that they be taught, and taught early in students' school careers, because lack of knowledge of Tier Two words—Stahl and Nagy's (2006) high-utility general words, Nation's (2001) academic words—is at the root of vocabulary and comprehension problems that leave students on the wrong side of Corson's lexical bar, unable to gain facility with higher status meaning systems of written language.

✳ What kinds of instructional methods are needed for ELLs?

First, there is very little research on vocabulary instruction for ELLs. Second, there is nothing in the research to suggest that what works with first-language learners does not work with second-language learners. Specifically, some of the most prominent second-language researchers have spoken to those two points.

Despite the importance of vocabulary to comprehension for English-language learners, there have been only four experimental studies conducted since 1980 examining the effectiveness of interventions designed to build vocabulary among language minority students learning English as a societal language. The findings indicate that research-based strategies used with first-language learners (National Reading Panel, 2000) are effective with second-language learners, although strategies must be adopted to the strengths and needs of second-language learners. (Calderon et al., 2005, p. 117)

These same authors noted that the instructional activities for their study of ELL vocabulary growth were based on "the vocabulary process developed by Beck and Colleagues (Beck, McKeown, & Kucan, 2002)" (p. 125). They went on to indicate that when words were introduced, the pronunciation of both the English and the Spanish words were provided, and when there was a Spanish cognate, that was pointed out. In bilingual classes the teacher used some Spanish to explain the meaning of some of the targeted Tier Two words.

What makes robust instruction effective for any student, whether ELL or native English speaking, is that students meet the words in multiple contexts and have ample opportunities to use and think about the words. The need for students, especially ELLs, to develop their vocabulary through using the words in extended talk is emphasized by many language scholars. For example, Corson (1995) asserts that in classrooms for first-language or ELL students, word learning takes place when students engage in purposeful talk with others that embeds the target words and displays their uses. Kowal and Swain's (1994) work with second-language students shows the need for conversation and discussion to provide the necessary elaboration to master rules of use of words across contexts. Dutro and Moran (2003) lay out guiding principles for English language instruction that include creating meaningful contexts for functional use of language and providing opportunities for practice and application.

The kinds of language interactions that characterize robust instructional activities provide the elaborated context availability that ELLs need. The focused and extended language input that is provided and output that is prompted by robust instruction benefit the development of language competence for first- and second-language learners.

CHAPTER 6

* * * * * * *

Extended Examples

In this chapter, we present examples of full lesson cycles for two texts and their associated set of target words. We consider them "extended" examples because we lay out the thinking process by which we considered and selected target words from the texts and developed specific instructional activities for the words.

One of the texts is a short selection that describes how trainers at an oceanarium in Florida responded to a threatening storm by moving dolphins and sea lions to hotel swimming pools: *Aquatic Guests* (Gaines, 2001). This selection is appropriate for fourth- and fifth-grade students. The other is a novel, *The View from Saturday,* a Newbery Award-winning book by E. L. Konigsburg (1998) that is appropriate for sixth-grade students.

EXTENDED EXAMPLE USING A SHORT TEXT SELECTION

We will start with the short selection *Aquatic Guests.* The full text is provided below. Please read it all the way through before going on to a description of the way we thought about and planned for a cycle of lessons related to words from the story.

Aquatic Guests
by Elizabeth P. Gaines

Since dawn, Elton Bolton, head trainer at Marine Life Oceanarium in Gulfport, Mississippi, had watched dark clouds spread ominously over the southeastern horizon. He kept his radio turned to the weather station. It was near the end of the 1985 hurricane season, and there were warnings that a dangerous storm called Elena, ripping over Florida for days, had entered the Gulf of Mexico. Heading northwest, it threatened the coast from Florida to central Louisiana.

Over the open water, Elena's winds increased to seventy-five miles per hour and covered an area of two hundred miles or more. Spiraling counterclockwise, the winds began to draw warm, moist air upward around a low pressure center—the eye of the hurricane. The winds could reach 125 miles per hour, and a roiling mound of water called a storm surge could be drawn up from the sea. A storm surge, somewhat like a tidal wave, is deadly. If one hit Marine Life, located on a narrow spit of land jutting into the Gulf, there was little doubt that the dolphins and sea lions in Elton's care would be in grave danger.

Elton calculated that, depending upon the unpredictable speed and direction the storm traveled, he would have less than a week to move the animals from Marine Life. But where would he move them? Except for those on the coast, there were no other sea life centers in the area equipped to handle twenty-one dolphins and seven sea lions.

Suddenly, Elton had an idea. Some five miles inland a number of motels had recently opened that were strongly built to withstand high winds. Perhaps the animals could be transported to these motels and live in their pools until the danger had passed. Elton quickly called the motel managers to ask about moving the dolphins and sea lions. As he had hoped, the managers were glad to help. "Only tell us how to prepare the pools," they said. "What about the chlorine? Can dolphins tolerate that?"

Elton instructed the managers to cut off the chlorine supply and let the water clear somewhat. He also asked that the guests stay away while he and his team worked with the animals. Any anxiety or stress could be fatal to the dolphins and sea lions.

Elton hurried to Marine Life, where workers were already boarding up windows. He told his trainers, Bill Corbin and Lloyd Lamy, about the plan to move the dolphins and sea lions. They knew just what to do. Bill hosed down a flatbed truck, and Lloyd filled a shallow tank on a second truck. Next the men brought heavy canvas slings from the storage room. The slings were six feet long and almost as wide, with the sides cut out for the dolphins' flippers. They inserted long poles into the wide side hems of the canvas, creating a sort of hammock.

A seven-foot dolphin circled Bill, ready to play any game. He nudged the sling with this snout and smiled his perpetual smile.

"Come on, Tarzan. Quit stalling. We're going for a ride, boy." Bill tried to maneuver the dolphin closer to the sling.

For a while Tarzan continued to play, but finally he seemed to sense the urgency in his trainer's voice. He swam to the edge of the pool and allowed the men to adjust the sling under him. Curious sea lions set up a raucous barking from their nearby tank.

Together Bill and Lloyd strained to lift Tarzan out of the pool. Water streamed from the sling. Suddenly the dolphin unexpectedly lunged and shifted his weight. Lloyd lost his grip on the sling and tumbled into the water. He grabbed for something, catching a flipper, and pulled Tarzan on top of him with a great splash.

At last Bill and Lloyd managed to load Tarzan into the sling and move him to the truck tank. The men laid a heavy tarpaulin over Tarzan and adjusted foam blocks and pads around him to protect the dolphin's sensitive skin and flippers. The wind whipped around the truck, chilling Bill and Lloyd to the bone, but the driving rain helped keep Tarzan's skin wet.

With Tarzan safely on the truck, Bill and Lloyd hurried back inside and, with some difficulty, loaded a sea lion onto the flatbed truck. They covered the animal with a wet tarpaulin and adjusted foam blocks around it.

Lloyd and Elton drove the two trucks through debris-strewn streets, heading for the first motel. Bill sat beside the sea lion in the back of the flatbed truck to keep it from falling off. Traffic was heavy as thousands of people evacuated the area, but at last they reached their destination. The trainers grabbed the poles of Tarzan's sling and carried him to the pool first. He slid into the water and swam about as if inspecting his new quarters. He showed his approval by emitting a series of clicking sounds. The sea lion soon joined him, and together they cavorted about. Children peeked through the motel room windows to watch as the sea animals checked into the Holiday Inn swimming pool.

Back at Marine Life, twenty volunteers had been working almost unceasingly over three days as the storm became more deadly. Elton, Lloyd, and Bill were glad for the help in transporting the rest of the dolphins and sea lions to various motels. Each trip was increasingly dangerous as live wires from fallen power poles lay in the streets. Pieces of rooftops sailed through the air. Trees were uprooted and branches ripped off. The hurricane heaved great waves shoreward, battering the waterfront in twenty-foot combers, a sign that a storm surge could be coming.

Finally, after hours of intense effort, the last of the dolphins was loaded, and the trucks headed for the road north. They were only a few miles inland when the hurricane roared over the beaches of Biloxi and Gulfport. Marine Life was overwhelmed by the advancing storm surge. The crest of its gigantic thirty-foot wave toppled and carried away practically everything in its path. Some buildings were swept from their foundations and dragged out to sea. Houses, cabins, and waterfront motels disintegrated before the fantastic energy of the storm surge.

When hurricane Elena finally moved on, the task of cleaning up the destruction began. Marine Life was heavily damaged, but luckily the foundation had held. Thanks to the hard work of Elton and his crew, all the animals were safe and sound. Their home took weeks to repair, and during that time the dolphins and sea lions resided in the motel pools, to the great delight of the other guests.

Which Words to Teach

Below we present our thoughts as we read through *Aquatic Guests* and considered which words we might want to teach from the selection. We present our thinking in the form of comments: first, our initial ideas as we came upon words that we thought would be unfamiliar and deserved consideration, and then our decisions about how to deal with the words.

Text	Vocabulary thoughts
Since dawn, Elton Bolton, head trainer at Marine Life Oceanarium[1] in Gulfport, Mississippi, had watched dark clouds spread ominously[2] over the southeastern horizon. He kept his radio turned to the weather station. It was near the end of the 1985 hurricane season, and there were warnings that a dangerous storm called Elena . . . had entered the Gulf of Mexico. Heading northwest, it threatened the coast from Florida to central Louisiana.	**1. Comment:** Many students will not know what an *oceanarium* is, and that ocean animals live there is important to the selection. **Decision:** Briefly explain that an *oceanarium* is like a zoo for animals who come from the ocean. Perhaps relate the word to *aquarium.* No further attention is needed because meaning is straightforward and application is limited.
Over the open water, Elena's winds increased to seventy-five miles per hour and covered an area of two hundred miles or more. Spiraling counterclockwise,[3] the winds began to draw warm, moist air upward around a low pressure center—the eye of the hurricane. The winds could reach 125 miles per hour, and a roiling mound of water called a storm surge could be drawn up from the sea. A storm surge . . . is deadly. If one hit [the] Marine Life Oceanarium, located on a narrow spit of land jutting into the Gulf, there was little doubt that the dolphins and sea lions in Elton's care would be in grave[4] danger.	**2. Comment:** One would not need to know the meaning of *ominously* to know that a storm is approaching. However, *ominously* is a great Tier Two word. **Decision:** *Ominously* is a candidate for inclusion in after-reading robust vocabulary instruction. **3. Comment:** It is not necessary to know the direction in which the winds are moving, but *counterclockwise* is a useful way to describe direction. **Decision:** Briefly explain that if something is moving counterclockwise, it is moving in the opposite direction than the hands of a clock move. No further attention is needed because meaning is straightforward. **4. Comment:** It is not necessary to know how serious the danger is, but *grave* is a good Tier Two word. **Decision:** *Grave* is a candidate for inclusion in after-reading vocabulary instruction.
Elton calculated[5] that, depending upon the unpredictable[6] speed and direction the storm traveled, he would have less than a week to move the animals from Marine Life. But where would he move them? Except for those on the coast, there were no other sea life centers in the area equipped to handle twenty-one dolphins and seven sea lions.	**5. Comment:** Many students may know the word *calculated* in a math context, so the use of *calculated* in a more general way would be useful. **Decision:** Briefly explain that *calculated* means figuring out something. No further attention is needed. **6. Comment:** Understanding that the time to move the animals is *unpredictable* is important because it adds to the *urgency* of the situation. But, even if *unpredictable* were unfamiliar, intermediate students know the base word, and the affixes *un-* and *-able* are among the easiest. **Decision:** Don't deal with *unpredictable*.

Text	Vocabulary thoughts
Suddenly, Elton had an idea. Some five miles inland a number of motels had recently opened that were strongly built to withstand high winds. Perhaps the animals could be transported to these motels and live in their pools until the danger had passed. Elton quickly called the motel managers to ask about moving the dolphins and sea lions. As he had hoped, the managers were glad to help. "Only tell us how to prepare the pools," they said. "What about the chlorine? Can dolphins tolerate[7] that?" Elton instructed the managers to cut off the chlorine supply and let the water clear somewhat. He also asked that the guests stay away while he and his team worked with the animals. Any anxiety[8] or stress could be fatal[9] to the dolphins and sea lions. Elton hurried to Marine Life, where workers were already boarding up windows. He told his trainers, Bill Corbin and Lloyd Lamy, about the plan to move the dolphins and sea lions. They knew just what to do. Bill hosed down a flatbed truck, and Lloyd filled a shallow tank on a second truck. Next the men brought heavy canvas slings from the storage room. The slings were six feet long and almost as wide, with the sides cut out for the dolphins' flippers. They inserted long poles into the wide side hems of the canvas, creating a sort of hammock. A seven-foot dolphin circled Bill, ready to play any game. He nudged the sling with this snout and smiled his perpetual[10] smile. "Come on, Tarzan. Quit stalling. We're going for a ride, boy." Bill tried to maneuver[11] the dolphin closer to the sling. For a while Tarzan continued to play, but finally he seemed to sense the urgency[12] in his trainer's voice. He swam to the edge of the pool and allowed the men to adjust the sling under him. Curious sea lions set up a raucous[13] barking from their nearby tank.	**7. Comment:** Whether dolphins can *tolerate* chlorine is important as an example of the kind of issues that had to be considered to save the dolphins. Additionally, *tolerate* is a good Tier Two word. **Decision:** Briefly explain that "Can dolphins tolerate that?" means "Can dolphins stand chlorine?" *Tolerate* is a candidate for after-reading robust instruction. **8, 9. Comment:** That *anxiety* and stress can be *fatal* to the animals is important to the kinds of issues that had to be considered to save the creatures. **Decision:** Briefly explain that *anxiety* means being worried, and something that is *fatal* is very serious and may cause death. No further attention is needed. **10, 11. Comment:** It is not necessary to know what *perpetual* and *maneuver* mean to understand the ideas, but both are excellent Tier Two words. **Decision:** *Perpetual* and *maneuver* do not need to be given attention during reading, but they are candidates for after-reading instruction. **12. Comment:** It is important to the pace with which the events are unfolding that Tarzan senses the *urgency*. **Decision:** Briefly explain that *urgency* is the need for something to be done right away. **13. Comment:** It is not necessary to know that the sea lions were acting *raucously*. But *raucous* is a good Tier Two word. **Decision:** *Raucous* and *urgency* are good candidates for after-reading instruction. *(cont.)*

Text	Vocabulary thoughts

Text

Together Bill and Lloyd strained to lift Tarzan out of the pool. Water streamed from the sling. Suddenly the dolphin unexpectedly lunged and shifted his weight. Lloyd lost his grip on the sling and tumbled into the water. He grabbed for something, catching a flipper, and pulled Tarzan on top of him with a great splash.

At last Bill and Lloyd managed to load Tarzan into the sling and move him to the truck tank. The men laid a heavy tarpaulin over Tarzan and adjusted foam blocks and pads around him to protect the dolphin's sensitive[14] skin and flippers. The wind whipped around the truck, chilling Bill and Lloyd to the bone, but the driving rain helped keep Tarzan's skin wet.

With Tarzan safely on the truck, Bill and Lloyd hurried back inside and, with some difficulty, loaded a sea lion onto the flatbed truck. They covered the animal with a wet tarpaulin and adjusted foam blocks around it.

Lloyd and Elton drove the two trucks through debris-strewn[15] streets, heading for the first motel. Bill sat beside the sea lion in the back of the flatbed truck to keep it from falling off. Traffic was heavy as thousands of people evacuated[16] the area, but at last they reached their destination.[17] The trainers grabbed the poles of Tarzan's sling and carried him to the pool first. He slid into the water and swam about as if inspecting his new quarters. He showed his approval by emitting[18] a series of clicking sounds.

The sea lion soon joined him, and together they cavorted[19] about. Children peeked through the motel room windows to watch as the sea animals checked into the Holiday Inn swimming pool.

Vocabulary thoughts

14. Comment: That care must be taken to protect the dolphin's skin and flippers is another example of the kind of issue the trainers had to deal with. But the reason that care is necessary is because dolphins have *sensitive* skin is not essential to the idea presented. *Sensitive* is a good Tier Two word.
Decision: Don't deal with *sensitive* during reading, but consider *sensitive* for after-reading instruction.

15. Comment: To get a sense of the conditions brought on by the hurricane it is useful to know what *debris-strewn* means.
Decision: Briefly explain that *debris-strewn* means that lots of pieces of things have fallen all over the place.

16. Comment: That people had to *evacuate* the area indicates how serious the storm was.
Decision: Briefly explain that *evacuated* means that everyone had to leave a place. *Evacuated* is a candidate for after-reading instruction.

17. Comment: From the context, it is likely that students will know that they reached some place.
Decision: Explanation of *destination* is not needed during reading, but *destination* is a good Tier Two word. *Destination* is a candidate for after-reading robust instruction.

18. Comment: Although students may not know what *emitting* means, the context will help them understand that it has to do with sounds.
Decision *Emitting* is a Tier Two word, but it is very narrow, so it will be excluded from after-reading vocabulary instruction.

Text	Vocabulary thoughts
Back at Maine Life, twenty volunteers had been working almost unceasingly over three days as the storm became more deadly. Elton, Lloyd, and Bill were glad for the help in transporting the rest of the dolphins and sea lions to various motels. Each trip was increasingly dangerous as live wires from fallen power poles lay in the streets. Pieces of rooftops sailed through the air. Trees were uprooted and branches ripped off. The hurricane heaved great waves shoreward, battering the waterfront in twenty-foot combers, a sign that a storm surge could be coming. Finally, after hours of intense effort, the last of the dolphins was loaded, and the trucks headed for the road north. They were only a few miles inland when the hurricane roared over the beaches of Biloxi and Gulfport. Marine Life was overwhelmed by the advancing storm.	**19. Comment:** The word *joined* in the text will let students know that the sea lion and dolphins were together. Students do not need to know that the animals *cavorted* about. But *cavorted* is a good Tier Two word. **Decision:** *Cavorted* is a candidate for after-reading instruction.
The crest of its gigantic thirty-foot wave toppled and carried away practically everything in its path. Some buildings were swept from their foundations and dragged out to sea. Houses, cabins, and waterfront motels disintegrated[20] before the fantastic energy of the storm surge. When hurricane Elena finally moved on, the task of cleaning up the destruction began. Marine Life was heavily damaged, but luckily the foundation had held. Thanks to the hard work of Elton and his crew, all the animals were safe and sound. Their home took weeks to repair, and during that time the dolphins and sea lions resided in the motel pools, to the great delight of the other guests.	**20. Comment:** The depth of the destruction is captured by the description that even motels *disintegrated.* **Decision:** Briefly explain that if something *disintegrates,* it breaks into many small pieces and is destroyed.

The kind of detailed explanations above are not meant as a model for teachers to emulate each time they go through a text to identify candidate words for robust instruction. Rather, the explicitness we provided is a way to reveal a kind of "mindset" of considerations. It has been our experience that when teachers have gained experience in identifying Tier Two words, their judgments are usually all that is needed.

Which Words to Teach: Final Decisions

As shown in the table above, we made comments about 20 words in *Aquatic Guests*. In the table below, we show that candidate set and then identify 11 of those words as our selection for after-reading robust vocabulary instruction. Here is how we thought about making our final selections. Upon examining the list, we immediately found two words that were very close in meaning. That is, *ominously* and *grave* each have serious negative connotations and if both are taught in close proximity it might cause confusion. Of the two, we prefer *ominously,* so we would omit *grave*. Similarly, *raucous* and *cavorted* both have a kind of a "carrying-on" connotation. Of the two, we prefer *cavorted,* so we would omit *raucous*. There is no other reason than personal preference to choose *ominously* and *cavorted* over *grave* and *raucous*. Others might choose differently. The point is that two words that have close meanings may cause some mix-up if they are included in the same instructional set.

Candidate set	Final set
ominously	*ominously*
grave	*tolerate*
tolerate	*perpetual*
perpetual	*maneuver*
maneuver	*urgency*
urgency	*sensitive*
raucous	*cavorted*
sensitive	
evacuated	
destination	
cavorted	

There are two other words that we've decided to eliminate from robust instruction: *evacuated* and *destination*. Both are reasonable Tier Two words, but compared to the other words on the list, their meanings and range of application are somewhat narrow: *evacuated* means "to leave a place that is not safe" and *destination* is "a place where people want to go." Given these decisions, there are now seven words in the final set as shown above.

When to Teach

We organize instruction around a teaching cycle that includes reading and discussing the text, introducing the words, follow-up activities over several days, and assessment. In the vocabulary work that we've done, we have introduced the words at a couple of different places early in the cycle. If a short text selection is being used, we may introduce all the words that same day—either right after reading or later in the day. Depending on how many words are being targeted, we might introduce, say, four of them on the day of story reading and another four on the next day. Or if the text read is longer, we might wait until Day 2 to introduce the vocabulary. All this is by way of saying that the timing of introducing the words after the story is read is flexible. Moreover, there may be two, three, or four follow-up days. What is important is that a set of target words (assuming 3 to 12, depending on the grade and instructional time provided) should have *at least* two separate days of follow-up instruction beyond the initial introduction. Days, of course, mean segments of separated time (say 10 to 30 minutes, depending on the number of words in a set).

How to Teach

Below we present a five-day cycle for the final set of words from *Aquatic Guests*. After the words are introduced, each subsequent day requires students to engage in activities designed to help them build a rich representation of word meanings.

The instructional cycle includes the use of some simple materials. You will need a card with each word on it to use during the lessons. Students will need a Vocabulary Log. (See Chapter 4, pp. 53–54.) The logs are usually included in activities on Days 3 and 4.

Day 1

The selection is read and discussed, and some words that are useful for understanding ideas in the text are briefly clarified in the course of reading (as indicated in this chapter on pp. 68–71), or, if that is not feasible, then briefly before reading.

Day 2

In the material that follows, we present introductions for each word, in which the following information is provided:

- the context in which each word appeared in the selection
- a student-friendly explanation
- an additional context beyond the one in which the word was used in the story
- an opportunity for students to interact with the word

As words are introduced, show the word card, pronounce the word, and be sure to give students ample opportunities to say the words during the lesson.

ominously

- In the selection, we read that the head trainer at an oceanarium had watched dark clouds spread *ominously* over the horizon. If something is *ominous*, it

looks frightening because it makes you think that something unpleasant is going to happen.
- An animal that shows you its teeth and growls has an *ominous* look.
- If I say something that might seem *ominous,* say "That's ominous!" If not, don't say anything. (In all cases it's important to ask students to explain why they responded as they did because making thinking public helps students make connections and integrate new learning with what they already know.)
  - hearing what sounds like wolves howling in the night
  - getting ready to go into a house that people say is haunted
  - falling into a puddle
  - being on a camping trip and hearing thunder
- What's the word that means "something seems scary because you think that something bad might happen"?

Notice that we changed the adverb *ominously* to the adjective *ominous.* When we prepare instructional materials, we readily change parts of speech when it enables us to develop good examples. Over the years, we have not seen students experience any difficulty with these alterations, nor have we had reports from teachers that such changes have caused students problems. In fact, we have observed students make such changes on their own without confusion.

tolerate

- In *Aquatic Guests,* when the trainers were thinking of moving the animals to hotel swimming pools, one of them wondered whether dolphins could *tolerate* the chlorine in swimming pools. If an animal or person can *tolerate* something it means that they can allow it to exist or happen.
- Some people can *tolerate* very loud music; other people cannot *tolerate* very loud music.
- If I say something that teachers would be likely to *tolerate,* say "They would tolerate that." If you think teachers would *not* tolerate something, say "No way!" For each response, students should be asked "why?" If students disagree, have them explain their reasons. Then, as the teacher, you can tell the students whether or not you would tolerate something.
  - if someone were late for school 10 times
  - if someone were late for school once
  - if someone said they didn't like the story they were reading
  - if someone said they would never do their homework
- What's the word that means "you think it's okay that something is the way it is"?

When we create these kinds of yes/no activities, sometimes either decision would be appropriate, depending on the thinking behind it. That is one reason why it is important to ask students to explain their responses. However, even when we've attempted to create clear positive and negative examples, a student might respond in an unexpected way for good reasons! For example, if a student responds "It's ominous" to falling into a puddle, and explains that "it might be really deep and you could drown," then he or she has done good thinking! But if he or she says, "because I don't like to get wet," then he or she needs to be reminded of the word's meaning.

perpetual

- Dolphins always look like they are smiling. That's why the dolphin, Tarzan, in *Aquatic Guests* is described as having a *perpetual* smile. Something that is *perpetual* never ends or changes.
- There's a *perpetual* flame that burns on President John Kennedy's grave; it never goes out.
- If I say something that is *perpetual*, say "perpetual." If not, don't say anything. Ask "why?"
  - a rainy day
  - the waves in the ocean
  - a story in yesterday's newspaper
  - the number line
- What's the word that means "never ending or changing"?

maneuver

- In the selection, one of the trainers tried to *maneuver* the dolphin closer to the sling. If you *maneuver* something, you move it to where you want it to be even though it is difficult to do.
- If you get a big refrigerator, the people who deliver it might have to *maneuver* it so it gets through your front door.
- If I say something that would require *maneuvering*, say "Maneuver it." If not, don't say anything. Ask "why?"
  - getting a big dog to go through a small dog door
  - putting a little box on a big table
  - driving a car down a hill
  - carrying packages of different sizes from a car to a porch
- What's the word that means "trying to get something somewhere even though it may be difficult"?

urgency

- In the article, the dolphin seemed to sense the *urgency* in his trainer's voice. Something that is *urgent* needs to be done immediately because it is very important.
- If someone sees smoke coming from a house, it is *urgent* that he call 911.

- If I say something that describes something that is urgent, say "Urgent." If not, don't say anything. Ask "why?"
  - stopping cars so they don't go over a broken bridge
  - clearing a runway so an airplane with medical supplies can take off
  - trying to get teams ready for a game at recess
  - keeping swimmers away from a beach where sharks have been sighted
- What's the word that means "something needs to be done at once"?

cavorted

- In *Aquatic Guests,* the dolphins and sea lions *cavorted* about. When someone *cavorts,* she runs and jumps around playfully.
- Little children *cavort* around a playground.
- If I say something that describes people or animals cavorting, say "Cavorting." If not, don't say anything. Ask "why?"
  - people in a wave pool
  - people in a library
  - dogs in a park
  - shoppers in a shoe store
- What's the word that means "moving around playfully"?

sensitive

- The trainers put pads around the dolphin to protect his *sensitive* skin and flippers. That means the dolphin's skin and flippers could be hurt easily. If something is *sensitive* it can be hurt easily.
- Things like your skin can be *sensitive,* or your nose may be *sensitive* to certain smells. *Sensitive* can also describe someone who responds strongly to other people's feelings. If you are *sensitive* to other people's problems and feelings, you understand them and are aware of them. A good baby-sitter is *sensitive* to a child's needs.
- If I say something that describes sensitivity, say "That's sensitive." If not, don't say anything. Ask "why?"
  - people with delicate skin
  - a girl who just got a cast off her arm
  - a student who brags about his new bike
  - someone who is friendly to a new student who seems shy
- What's the word that can mean "understanding how others feel"?

Notice that we provided two senses of the word *sensitive* because both meanings are related and because both meanings are commonly encountered in conversation and text.

Day 3

Ask students to respond to the following questions and to explain their choices:

- Would someone show fear or joy if they saw something *ominous*?
- Is *tolerate* more like letting something go on or trying to stop it?
- If something is in *perpetual* motion, does it never start or never stop?
- Is *maneuver* more like figuring something out or asking someone to do something for you?
- If something is *urgent,* should you ignore it or try to do something about it?
- Is *cavorting* more like eating or dancing?
- Would a *sensitive* person make fun of others?

Have students form small groups of three or four, and ask each group to create a list based on brainstorming about several of the items below. We have found it best to assign about three words to each group, also making sure that each item is given to at least two groups. Then the groups can compare their responses.

- Come up with some situations that you cannot *tolerate.*
- Describe some *ominous* situations.
- Imagine some conditions or circumstances that you wish could be *perpetual.*
- Describe situations in which people might need to *maneuver.*
- Decide on situations that could be described as *urgent.*
- Give examples of times when *cavorting* would not be appropriate.
- Find out what kinds of foods or medicines or conditions people in the group or their pets are *sensitive* to.

When the groups finish their brainstorming, lead a discussion in which each group explains their ideas to the rest of the class.

Have students work with a partner to develop a friendly explanation for each vocabulary word, and write it in their Vocabulary Logs. To develop their explanations, students should talk over with their partners how they remember the word being described and the contexts in which it has been used. They can also consult dictionaries if they would like. Check that students are recording good explanations into their logs. If needed, you might want to share a sample explanation with the class for each word because the log is a permanent record for the students and the explanations should be strong.

Day 4

Ask students to match one of the words with each of the following comments:

- "Will this ever end?"
- "That sounded like the wind is getting wilder."
- "Alright, you can do that."
- "Maybe we need to turn it sideways."
- "Get help now!"
- "Better wear sunscreen and a hat out there today."
- "Catch that Frisbee!"

Ask students to complete the sentence stems. Go over them together and then have students write a strong sentence for each word in their Vocabulary Logs:

- In a land of *perpetual* darkness, people . . .
- Because the bus driver cannot *tolerate* any *cavorting*, riders . . .
- The nurse showed that she was *sensitive* to how the little girl with the broken arm felt by . . .
- We could tell that it was an *urgent* situation because the crossing guard told us . . .
- In a race, runners have to *maneuver* as they work their way around the track because . . .
- An *ominous* sight in a forest might be seeing . . .

To encourage students to think about the vocabulary words outside of the classroom, challenge them with these activities:

- Ask students to look for examples of *maneuvering* on their way home from school.
- Have students find in a television program they are watching or a book they are reading an *urgent* situation and an *ominous* situation. Tell them to be prepared to discuss what is different between the two types of situations.
- Have students find in a book, television program, or newspaper a situation where someone is *sensitive*—or failed to be *sensitive* when he or she needed to be.

Day 5

As an engaging way to review the vocabulary before the test, tape a word card with a vocabulary word on it under each student's desk. Have students "discover" their cards and then provide the class with a sentence or explanation for the word.

As assessments for the words, we provide two formats. One is a straightforward common "objective" assessment: true/false. The second assessment goes beyond identifying whether a statement is correct or not. It requires generating an explanation. You might want to do one or both, depending upon what you want to know about students' knowledge of the words.

True or False

- If a situation is *perpetual*, you will just have to *tolerate* it.
- If your dog likes to *cavort* in the snow, you know that she is not *sensitive* to the cold.
- If you are trying to *maneuver* through a crowded room, you will probably have to go in more than one direction to get through.
- If a situation is *urgent*, you can take your time to think about making a decision.
- If you have an *ominous* feeling, you are probably laughing.

Complete the Sentences

- The *perpetual* noise from the jackhammer caused . . .
- When the farmer saw the two puppies *cavorting* in the henhouse . . .
- Charlene showed her *sensitivity* to her new classmate when . . .
- Henry and his mother figured they could *maneuver* the piano by . . .
- When he called me I could tell that the situation was *urgent* because . . .
- It's an *ominous* sign when you turn on your computer and . . .

EXTENDED EXAMPLE USING A NOVEL WITH MANY TIER TWO WORDS

Many reading/language arts teachers choose to complement the reading of short stories and excerpts often found in basal anthologies with opportunities for their students to read complete novels. In this section, we provide an example of vocabulary instruction based on words selected from a novel that is often read by sixth graders.

The novel is *The View from Saturday,* a Newbery Award-winning book by E. L. Konigsburg (1998). Konigsburg's novel focuses on four sixth graders who become their school's academic bowl representatives and their teacher who prepares them for the competition.

The View from Saturday is 160 pages long. There are 12 chapters or sections in the novel, but these are unequal in length. It seems reasonable to assume that students will be able to read and discuss 15–20 pages of the novel each day. This would allow us to deal with the whole novel over a period of 2 weeks. Week 1 would focus on Chapters 1–3 (pp. 1–93). Week 2 would focus on Chapters 4–12 (pp. 94–160). The novel is rich in the word choices made by the author, providing memorable contexts for Tier Two words.

Which Words to Teach

There are many words in *The View from Saturday* that are candidates for robust vocabulary instruction. Our question, then, was which words will both enhance students' vocabulary development and support their understanding and appreciation of the novel. Below is a list of the words we initially considered as Tier Two words with mileage, with the words that we finally chose in boldface.

Chapters 1–3	Chapters 4–12
Chapter 1 **benevolently** bated maimed **ironic**	*Chapter 4* suppressed **spontaneous** **admonish** contenders
Chapter 2 precision diversity incandescently ecology hovering **subtle** **preoccupied** **sarcasm** **philosophical** frenzy	*Chapter 5* **malice** equivalent quaint vulgar *Chapter 6* trounce **profound** **confided** **mediocre** vanquished jubilant
Chapter 3 **nonchalantly** itinerant accessible **inevitable** confined brisk verge defective	*Chapter 7* random pretext **unprecedented** **arrogance**
	Chapter 8 unison adorn
	Chapter 9 precedent
	Chapter 11 **perpetual**

We made our final selections based on a number of factors. Some words were closely related to important themes in the novel, such as *ironic* and *inevitable,* which describe how several seemingly unconnected events played out. *Malice* (malicious) relates to the way some of the characters were treated as well as to how some characters acted in order to thwart another character's plans. *Mediocre* and *arrogance* describe the performance and attitude of some of the students involved in the competition. The words *sarcasm, philosophical,* and *nonchalantly* are words we thought that sixth graders would have heard but probably would not have a rich understanding of. Some of the candidates, like *spontaneous,* appeared more than once in the text. Some of the words were related, such that teaching one would also support students in understanding the other—for example, *unprecedented* and *precedent.* We also thought about how the words were distributed across the novel, so that the words we selected were not all in just one part of the book. Finally, some of the words that we chose were simply ones that we thought were the more interesting Tier Two words.

We selected eight words for each week. That seemed to be a realistic number for students to learn well, and also provided enough words to create interesting activities. But at the sixth-grade level there can be more than eight words per week.

When to Teach

On the first day of instruction we would have students read Chapter 1 and then we follow up that reading with an introduction to the words. This means that on the first day students would also be introduced to some words in Chapters 2 and 3, which they will not have read yet. We suggest this departure from our usual tactic of teaching words after they have been encountered in text because we want to introduce the full set of words early in the week so that students will have a chance to interact with the words several times during the week.

If eight words seems like a lot to introduce at one time—keeping with our point earlier in this chapter that the scheduling of the cycle of activities should be flexible—another possibility is to introduce four words at one time during the day and four at another time. Or introduce four words right after the first chapter has been completed and the other four on the next day.

How to Teach

A five-day instructional cycle follows for each set of words for the book. As in this previous example, you'll need a card for each word and students will use Vocabulary Logs.

Week 1

Day 1

In the instruction that follows we provide our usual steps for introducing a word: the context in which each word appeared in the selection, a student-friendly explanation, an additional context beyond the one in which the word was used in the novel, and an opportunity for students to interact with the word. As words are introduced, show the word card, pronounce the word, and be sure to give students ample opportunities to say the words during the lesson.

benevolently

- In Chapter 1, we read that the judge smiled *benevolently* over the audience at the regional championship. If someone is *benevolent,* he or she is kind and wants the best for everyone.
- A *benevolent* principal would be very understanding and willing to help students.
- If I say something that might seem *benevolent,* say "That's benevolent!" If not, don't say anything. Recall that it is very important to ask students to explain why they responded as they did because making thinking public helps students make connections and integrate new learning with what they already know.
  - offering to help someone move into their new house
  - ignoring a person who is having trouble lifting a suitcase
  - interrupting someone who is trying to explain her problem
  - asking someone if he has a ride home from the game
  - What's the word that means "someone is acting in a kind and helpful way"?

ironic

- In Chapter 1, Noah's Narrative, we read about Allen Diamondstein, who said that it was *ironic* that his father was getting married just as he was getting divorced. An *ironic* situation is odd or kind of funny because there is a connection between things that seem opposite in some way. The connection is usually something that you would not want, like catching the flu on the first day of vacation—because you can't go out and play on a day that you should be able to.
- It would be *ironic* if someone gave you a new seat for your bike when you had just sold it.
- If I say something that might seem *ironic,* say "That's so ironic!" If not, don't say anything. Ask "why?"
  - offering someone some sticky taffy when she just came back from getting a filling at the dentist
  - finding out the movie you have been waiting for is finally coming to a local theater
  - giving someone a DVD when his DVD player just broke
  - finding out that the newspaper route that you wanted so you could make money in the summer will not be available until the fall
- What's the word that means "connected in a way that you would not expect"?

subtle

- In Chapter 2, Nadia's Narrative, we will read about Ethan who describes the star's performance in *The Phantom of the Opera* as *subtle.* Something that is *subtle* is not obvious or "in your face." It's more complicated and interesting and takes some thinking about. A *subtle* remark might seem simple on the surface, but it could be very meaningful if you think more about it.

- A design on a shirt that you can only see if you get really close to it would be *subtle*.
- Explain how each of the following could be subtle or not subtle. Ask "why?"
  - the scent of perfume
  - the choice of colors for painting a house
  - the way a song moves between verses and a refrain
  - the choices made by a gardener in planting flowers that will bloom in the spring
- What's the word that means "something that is not obvious"?

preoccupied

- In Chapter 2, Nadia suggests that her father was so *preoccupied* with what time it was that he didn't even notice her remark about his very important appointment. If someone is *preoccupied*, he or she is thinking about something so much that he or she doesn't pay attention to other things.
- Someone who is playing a video game can be so *preoccupied* that she forgets to stop for lunch.
- If I say something that could *preoccupy* someone, say "Could be preoccupied." If not, don't say anything. Ask "why?"
  - practicing for a race
  - reading a novel that you don't really care much about
  - thinking about your next move in a chess game
  - choosing from a menu at a restaurant where you go every week
- What's the word that means "someone is not aware of what's going on because he or she is thinking about something"?

sarcastic

- In Chapter 2, the remark that Nadia's father doesn't notice is described as *sarcastic*. Nadia said, "I'm sure it's an important appointment," when she really meant that it was probably *not* so important. When someone says something *sarcastic,* he says the opposite of what he means, usually as a way to show that he doesn't like something.
- It would be *sarcastic* if someone said "Oh good!—chicken for dinner!" when she had just eaten chicken for three days in a row and was really tired of it.
- If I say something that could be a *sarcastic* comment, say "That's sarcastic." If not, don't say anything. Ask "why?"
  - "There's a real all-star player" after a baseball player makes two errors
  - "That was really worth the money" after seeing a fantastic movie

- "I'm so glad I bought this watch" after your new watch stops working
- "She's a great role model" after a pop star gets arrested for shoplifting
- What's the word that means "you really don't mean what you say"?

philosophical

- In Chapter 2, when Nadia and her father talk about the newly hatched turtles, he says: "What comes ashore always washes back out. That's not a *philosophical* statement, Nadia. It's a fact." Nadia's father is contrasting factual information with ideas that are *philosophical* or abstract. Philosophers think about big questions that don't have clear answers like "What is real?" and "How do we know that we know something?"
- A teacher might say that someone is being *philosophical* if she asks what homework is good for anyway.
- If I say something that might interest a *philosophical* person, say "That's quite philosophical." If not, don't say anything. Ask "why?"
  - trying to figure out what life would be like without a system for telling time
  - the batting average of your favorite baseball player
  - the population of your town
  - thinking about whether a person is aware before he or she is born
- What's the word that means "focusing on big questions or ideas rather than facts"?

nonchalantly

- In Chapter 3, we will read how Ethan got on the bus, put his knapsack on the seat beside him, and then *nonchalantly* put his leg over it. He was trying to make it difficult for anyone to sit next to him, but he didn't want to be too obvious about it. If you're doing something *nonchalantly,* you are calm and trying not to draw attention to yourself.
- You might *nonchalantly* start moving toward the door if you wanted to leave a party early.
- If I say something that could be done *nonchalantly,* say "Cool." If not, don't say anything. Ask "why?"
  - painting a fence
  - dropping a note on someone's desk
  - moving next to someone you want to meet
  - running away from a snake
- What's the word that means "trying to be cool so no one notices what you're doing"?

inevitable

- In Chapter 3, we will read that when Ethan finally gets off the bus, he sees the *inevitable*: Julian is waiting for him. If something is *inevitable,* it is certain to happen and cannot be prevented.
- It is *inevitable* that if people don't take their cars in for regular maintenance, they will need car repairs at some point.
- If I say something that is *inevitable,* say "That's inevitable." If not, don't say anything. Ask "why?"
    - more daylight hours in the summer
    - lots of sales for a new soft drink
    - high tides followed by low tides on an ocean shore
    - winning a spelling bee after much studying
- What's the word that means "it's bound to take place"?

Day 2

Prompt students to think about some features of each word's meaning by responding to the following questions:

- If something is *inevitable,* should you make plans to prevent it? Why or why not?
- Would a *benevolent* person be likely to ignore a cry for help? Why or why not?
- Is *philosophical* more like getting the details or thinking about the bigger picture? Why?
- If someone is *preoccupied,* would he be likely to hear what's going on around him? Explain.
- If someone is acting *nonchalantly,* would you be likely to notice what she is doing? Explain.
- Could the comment "Boy, I love this song!" ever be said in a *sarcastic* way? Explain.
- Would it be *ironic* if someone got a bus pass just when the bus drivers went on strike? Why or why not?
- If something is *subtle,* would you be able to understand it without thinking about it much? Explain.

Have students work in groups to develop contexts or examples about each word by responding to the following:

- What could be *ironic* about wanting a snow day and waking up to find out that it snowed 12 inches during the night?
- Name something that is *inevitable* every day in your life, and explain.

- Think of something that a coach might say in a *sarcastic* tone of voice.
- Tell about someone whom you think of as *benevolent*.
- When might you act *nonchalantly*? Why?
- If someone is *philosophical,* what might she like to do?
- Name something that you could describe as *subtle* and explain why.
- What might *preoccupy* a chef?

Let each group share their responses and discuss them.

Day 3

Completing analogies is often included in sixth-grade language arts standards. On page 93, the end of Chapter 3 in the novel, Julian uses an analogy to explain what the term *chops* means. So we think it's an especially appropriate activity here. Have students complete the following analogies:

- Someone who is *benevolent* is not mean or selfish; someone who is *preoccupied* is not . . . (possible responses: focused, attentive).
- Something *ironic* is *unexpected*; something *inevitable* is . . . (possible responses: certain, unavoidable).
- Something *subtle* is not *obvious or "in your face"*; something *philosophical* is not . . . (possible responses: factual, concrete).
- If you are acting *nonchalantly,* you are trying hard not to be noticed; if you are being *sarcastic,* you are trying hard not to be . . . (possible responses: straightforward, honest, saying what you really mean).

Have students work with a partner to craft other analogies with these pairs of vocabulary words:

- benevolent   sarcastic
- ironic   nonchalantly
- subtle   preoccupied
- inevitable   philosophical

Have sets of partners write the incomplete analogies (i.e., omitting the last part) on cards, and then switch with another pair of students to see if they can complete them correctly.

Review the words' meanings by having students create an explanation for each word. Discuss the explanations that students propose and decide on those that include the most complete information about each word. Have students write those explanations in their Vocabulary Logs.

Day 4

Have students work together in pairs to complete the sentence stems below. When students are done, have the pairs share their work in a whole-group discussion to ensure that the sentences are strong contexts. Ask students to write the sentences in their Vocabulary Logs.

- Jason tries to be *nonchalant* when he . . .
- The design on Shari's party invitation was *subtle* because . . .
- Fred can be described as a *philosophical* person because . . .
- Our gym teacher can be described as *benevolent* because . . .
- If someone is *preoccupied* with swimming, then . . .
- Our teacher thought it was *ironic* that everyone wanted . . .
- After losing a basketball game, a player might make a *sarcastic* remark like . . .
- The change of seasons on Earth is *inevitable* because . . .

A valuable activity for prompting thinking about the words involves challenging students to find other examples from the novel that could be described by the vocabulary words. The power of this kind of activity is that it combines vocabulary interactions with comprehension work—giving students a chance to thoughtfully consider the text in a new light.

Pose the following questions and have students work in small groups to reread sections of the novel and provide responses.

- In Chapter 1, Noah describes all the activities associated with preparations for Izzy Diamondstein and Margaret Draper's wedding. Select the activities that involve *benevolence.*
- In Chapter 2, Nadia makes some *sarcastic* remarks. Find some examples.
- In Chapter 2, Nadia's father asks her about what the turtles do between the time they leave the Sargasso Sea and the time they come back to mate 15 years later. Nadia discovers a *subtle* connection between her life and the life of the turtles. What does she come to realize?
- Are there any other *subtle* similarities between the turtles and Nadia? Or between the turtles and any of the other characters? Describe them.
- In Chapters 1, 2, and 3, Noah, Ethan, Nadia, and Julian discover that they are connected to one another in unexpected ways. Describe these *ironic* relationships.
- List the characters in Chapters 1–3 and what they are *preoccupied* with.

To encourage students to think about the vocabulary words outside of the classroom, challenge them with these activities:

- Bring in examples of advertisements or illustrations on book covers or CDs that convey *subtle* messages and explain.
- Share examples of songs with *philosophical* lyrics.
- Find examples of *ironic* images in artwork. As an example, display Chris Van Allsburg's *The Mysteries of Harris Burdick* (1984), which includes illustrations of scenes and events that are inconsistent or unexpected, such as birds flying away from the wallpaper on which they are painted and a vine growing out of a book.

Day 5

To review the vocabulary before the test, prepare multiple cards with one vocabulary word on each. Have students select a word card from a box and provide an explanation for the word. To encourage thoughtful explanations, we have had the other students give a "thumbs up" or a "thumbs down" to indicate that a student's explanation was adequate or not adequate. Students who got a "thumbs down" got another chance to provide a better explanation, or they could call on a volunteer to do so.

Below we provide two types of assessments. The first is a true/false test, which, as we mentioned in Chapter 3, allows students a 50% chance of getting a right answer. It could be made much more challenging by asking students to explain why each item is true or false. The second assessment asks for written responses that require students to develop or explain a context for the word.

True or False

- A person who is trying to be *nonchalant* about something would want people to notice what she was doing.
- If something is *subtle,* you would probably notice it right away.
- Someone who has a hobby could become *preoccupied* with it.
- A *philosophical* person might decide to take some time off from work to just read and think for a while.
- A *sarcastic* remark can be hurtful.
- A police officer who stops traffic to let a turtle cross the road would be acting *benevolently.*
- Finding out that the trick you wanted to play on someone had just been played on you would be an example of *irony.*
- It is *inevitable* that if you work hard you will be famous.

Sentence Stems

- Jeff was trying to be *subtle* when he said . . .
- It is hard to be *nonchalant* when . . .
- I couldn't resist being *sarcastic* when my sister told me . . .
- My teacher said I sounded *philosophical* when I told her . . .

- The scene in the movie was *ironic* because . . .
- The most *inevitable* thing about dinner at my house is . . .
- When you see a homeless person, it would be *benevolent* to . . .
- Driving while *preoccupied* . . .

Week 2

Day 1

Introduce the words after reading and talking about Chapter 4 in the novel. As noted previously, you may want to introduce four words at one time and then four at another time. Display a word card for each of the eight target words and discuss each as indicated below:

spontaneous

- In Chapter 4, after the Epiphany Team was awarded six points, there was a *spontaneous* burst of applause. When something is *spontaneous*, it is done without planning or thinking ahead about it.
- You might *spontaneously* begin to sing along if you were in the car and your favorite song was played.
- If I say something that might be *spontaneous*, say "That's spontaneous." If not, don't say anything. Ask "why?"
  - preparing for a piano recital
  - yawning when you're bored
  - dressing up for a special occasion
  - buying a new coat because you pass a store that advertises a big one-day-only sale
- So what's the word that means "spur-of-the-moment"?

admonish

- In Chapter 4, the judge had to *admonish* the audience during the competition by telling them not to applaud because it was distracting to the contestants. To *admonish* someone means to caution or scold him or her in a mild way. If students are talking too loudly in the cafeteria, they could be *admonished* for their behavior.
- If I say something that someone might be *admonished* for, say "You'll get admonished." If not, don't say anything. Ask "why?"
  - forgetting to take out the trash
  - helping a new student find her locker
  - practicing your yodeling early in the morning
  - finding a lost key
- What's the word that means "advised to change what you're doing"?

malice

- In Chapter 5, we will read that during the performance of *Annie,* students dis-rupted the show by yelling "Arf! Arf!" whenever Sandy the dog was on stage. Mrs. Olinsky thought that "this was not mischief. There is a playful quality to mischief. This was malice. There is a mean quality to *malice.* Someone in her class was terribly mean."
- If you show *malice* toward someone, you deliberately do something mean or hurtful. It would be *malicious* to purposely leave a dog in a car with no win-dows open on a hot day.
- If I say something that could be malicious, say "That's malicious." If not, don't say anything. Ask "why?"
  - not giving someone an important message that has been entrusted to you
  - asking someone to tell you about their science project that won first prize in a science fair
  - hiding someone's lunch
  - telling your friends about a story in the newspaper about your teacher's wedding
- Let's say the word that means "being mean."

profound

- We will read in Chapter 6 that for many teachers at Epiphany the sixth grad-ers' performance in the competition was a *profound* victory. Something *pro-found* is very significant and deeply felt.
- Meeting someone that you admire or look up to can be a *profound* experience.
- If I say something that might be *profound,* say "That's profound." If not, don't say anything. Ask "why?"
  - listening to a poem that seems to be about feelings that you have experi-enced
  - discovering that you have to get a flu shot
  - reading a letter that your grandmother wrote to your mother when she was graduating from high school
  - voting in a national election for the first time
- What's the word that means "really gets to you"?

confided

- In Chapter 6, we will read that Mrs. Sharkey, the math teacher, *confided* to Ms. Masolino, the music teacher, that for the first time in the history of Epiphany Middle School there was a chance that the sixth graders might beat the sev-enth graders.

- If you *confide* in someone, you share a secret with him or her or discuss something privately.
- You might *confide* your fears about an upcoming competition by talking them over with your friend.

Note: *Confide* presents an opportunity to introduce some morphologically related words that students might either be familiar with or are likely to encounter. Thus, on a subsequent day (i.e., after the word has been worked with), you might have a brief conversation such as: "We learned that confide means 'to share your ideas in a private way.' If you were given information that was labeled as confidential, would you expect it to be available for anyone to read? Explain. If someone were described as a good confidant, how would you expect them to act, or what would you expect them to do?"

- If any of the situations sound like times you'd want to confide in someone, say "I'd confide." If not, don't say anything. Ask "why?"
  - trying to sort out your feelings about a failing grade
  - sharing your ideas about a project that you are working on with a group
  - expressing your feelings about a friend who has let you down
  - telling a mother about your experiences baby-sitting in the hopes that she will hire you
- What's the word that means "telling something private"?

mediocre

- In Chapter 7, we will read that Mrs. Sharkey said that the current seventh graders were only *mediocre,* even when they were doing their very best. If you describe someone or something as *mediocre,* you mean that he or she or it is ordinary, not special in any way.
- If a movie is *mediocre,* it is not really great or awful.
- Explain how or why each of the following might be described as mediocre or as anything but mediocre.
  - a garden
  - a bookstore
  - a pair of boots
  - a TV show
- What's the word that means "not that interesting or exciting"?

unprecedented

- In Chapter 7, all the buzz was that to have a sixth-grade team make it to the district finals was an *unprecedented* accomplishment. Something *unprecedented* has never happened before. There is no *precedent* or example of such a thing ever taking place. The first time a woman is elected president of the United States will be described as an "unprecedented event."

Note: The word *precedent* appears in Chapter 9. When it is encountered, it would make sense to draw students' attention to it and to its relationship to *unprecedented.* You might begin by telling them that the words *precedent* and *unprecedented* are related to the word *precede,* which means "to come before."

- If I say something that might be *unprecedented,* say "That's unprecedented!" If not, don't say anything. Ask "why?"
  - The local high school is chosen to host an American Idol regional competition.
  - The middle school soccer team is scheduled to play some games at their home field and some games at the fields of other schools.
  - All students in your town are invited to visit the White House.
  - The teachers in your school district attend a professional workshop and students do not attend class.
- What's the word that means "for the very first time"?

arrogance

- In Chapter 7, we will find out that the Knightsbridge team was known for its *arrogance. Arrogant* persons act as if they are better than anyone else. They are conceited.
- A student who thinks she will always achieve the highest score on tests might be *arrogant.*
- If I say someone who might be described as *arrogant,* say "How arrogant!" If not, don't say anything. Ask "why?"
  - someone who constantly brags about his athletic ability
  - someone who is curious and likes to listen to the stories people tell
  - someone who keeps talking about her great report and the fabulous comments that her teacher made about it
  - someone who likes to keep up to date on his favorite musical group's concert schedule
- What's the word that means "think you're better than everyone else"?

Day 2

Ask students to figure out which of their words goes with the following scenarios. What word could you use to describe:

- something that just burst into flames
- your football team wins more games than it ever has

- a book that affected you so much you read it three times
- playing a trick on someone to make her cry
- an outfit that was neither gorgeous nor dreadful
- someone who thought she was too good to say hello to her classmates
- what a neighbor might do if you were playing your music too loud
- telling someone your greatest wish and asking him not to tell anyone else

Ask students to make "idea substitutions" in the following sentences by rewording the sentence so that it contains one of their words. Use the first one as an example by reading the sentence, then telling them which word they should use to say the same thing as the sentence. If needed, give them the sentence provided. For the rest of the items, just give them the sentence.

- It was one for the record books: every player on the team got a home run in the same game. (*unprecedented*)
- The fifth graders were so tired of the sixth graders showing off their trophy from the spelling bee that they just ignored them. (*arrogant*)
- It is really fun to do things just because you suddenly feel like it. (*spontaneous*)
- The policeman told the bike riders that they should not be riding without helmets. (*admonish*)
- The lunch served in the school cafeteria isn't bad—but then again, it's not good either. (*mediocre*)
- The book I read last week really made me think hard about life. (*profound*)
- When you feel upset about something, it really helps to be able to talk to someone about it. (*confide*)
- Deliberately giving somebody the wrong information when he asks for directions would be kind of cruel. (*malicious*)

Day 3

Have students create an explanation for each word's meaning and write it in their Vocabulary Logs. Discuss the explanations that students propose and decide on those that include the most complete information about each word.

Have students think about possible relationships between the words below by responding to the question containing each word pair. Have students explain their answers as fully as they can, including possibly providing examples. Help students see that the questions could be answered in different ways. Use the first two as examples:

- *arrogant/unprecedented*
  Could something *unprecedented* make someone *arrogant*? For example, a person could become *arrogant* if she did something *unprecedented*

because she might be so proud of herself for doing something for the first time.

- *spontaneous/malicious*

  Would something *spontaneous* be *malicious*? For example, something that is *spontaneous* would not be malicious because you have to intend to hurt someone if you're *malicious,* and something *spontaneous* happens without any planning.

- *admonish/malice*

  Would you *admonish* someone for something that showed *malice*?

- *mediocre/profound*

  Could something *mediocre* be *profound*?

- *arrogant/mediocre*

  Could someone who is *arrogant* be a *mediocre* student?

- *confide/profound*

  Would you want to *confide* a *profound* idea that you had?

- *unprecedented/mediocre*

  Could something *unprecedented* be *mediocre*?

- *confide/arrogant*

  Would you want to *confide* in someone who is *arrogant*?

- *admonish/spontaneous*

  Why would someone be *admonished* for doing something that was *spontaneous*?

Day 4

Ask students to name the vocabulary word that goes with each of these comments:

- "That was so mean!"
- "Ooh, deep, man, really deep."
- "Unbelievable! That's never happened before!"
- "The principal wasn't too happy when we came in late."
- "That joke wasn't really that funny."
- "He thinks he's a gift to the planet!"
- "Please keep this information to yourself!"
- "What just happened?"

Have students work in pairs or groups to complete the following table that asks them to think about how different people would perform actions or say things that relate to the vocabulary words.

	chef	robber	singer
Why might a . . . act *arrogant*?			
What would a . . . do that was *unprecedented*?			
What might a . . . do that showed *malice*?			
How could a . . . be *spontaneous*?			
How would a . . . *admonish* someone?			
What would a . . . do that was *mediocre*?			
What could a . . . say that was *profound*?			
What might a . . . *confide*?			

Day 5

To review the vocabulary words before the test, make multiple copies of cards for each word and insert one into each student's copy of *The View from Saturday*. Ask students to look in their books to find the card, and then explain the meaning of the word written on it.

Below are some test items that we would provide for students to complete. We again provide two formats. The first requires associating a word with a comment that represents the word's meaning. The second taps a deeper level of knowledge by requiring students to generate an explanation. One or both could be used, depending upon what you want to know about students' knowledge of the words.

Write the Vocabulary Word That Best Matches Each Comment Below

- "Please do not throw paper away unless you have used both sides."
- "That's never been done before!"
- "I have something to talk over with you in private."
- "If I'm in the contest, no one else will have a chance to win."
- "I will never forget how that extraordinary day changed my life."
- "I wouldn't recommend going to that movie unless you just want to waste some time."
- "That's a great idea! Let's go right now!"
- "He planned the whole thing just to hurt my feelings."

Answer the Questions

- Why would a *spontaneous* reaction be an honest one?
- If you wanted to *confide* in someone, why would you choose a place where others could not overhear your conversation?

- How could athletes in the Olympics achieve *unprecedented* records in their events?
- Why would a person known for *malicious* behavior not be *profoundly* admired by others?
- Why would a player be *admonished* by her coach if she was only putting forth a *mediocre* effort?
- Why aren't people with an *arrogant* attitude very popular?

NOVELS WITH FEW TIER TWO WORDS

The View from Saturday (Konigsburg, 1998) as well as the novels listed in Appendix B provide evidence that many novels for children and young adults are excellent sources of Tier Two words. However, there are also many novels that are not as good sources for such words. For example, there are only a few Tier Two words in the well-loved novel *Sarah, Plain and Tall* (MacLachlan, 1985). This is understandable because the story is narrated by a child, Anna.

Some Tier Two words in *Sarah, Plain and Tall* include *wretched, pesky, feisty, pungent, eerie,* and *prim.* To supplement these, we would choose words that could be used in talking and writing about the novel. For example, before Sarah comes, the children feel *forlorn,* or lonely and unhappy. Sarah is not *intimidated,* or made to feel afraid, by the haystack, or by the work on the farm, or even by Jacob's silences. Anna, Caleb, and Jacob feel great *suspense,* or worry and tension, as they wait for Sarah to return from her trip into town. The prairie meadows are *vast,* or very large or great in size.

Another popular novel with a limited number of Tier Two words is *Hatchet* (Paulsen, 1987). Some Tier Two words that appear early in the book include *remnants, abating, asset, ruefully, dormant,* and *exulted.* In later chapters, the following Tier Two words are possible choices for instruction: *incessant, intact, stymied,* and *frenzied.* Other Tier Two words that do not appear in the novel can be used to talk about the book and Brian, its main character. For example, *predicament* aptly describes the situation Brian finds himself in after his plane crashes. *Contradictory* can be used for the "up-and-down feelings" that Brian endures throughout his difficult and painful experience or *ordeal.* Both the sun and the mosquitoes might be characterized as *unrelenting* or *relentless* because they are so unyielding and harsh. Brian demonstrates profound resourcefulness or *ingenuity* as he *devises* ways to secure food and shelter as well as protect himself from animals on the island.

These two examples demonstrate how to enhance the experience of reading a novel by selecting words to teach that capture critical aspects of plot, setting, and character, and provide students with interesting and precise ways to think and talk about them.

CHAPTER 7

∗ ∗ ∗ ∗ ∗ ∗ ∗

Professional Development

Our motivation for this chapter is to give readers opportunities to systematically try their hand at thinking through and developing the kinds of activities we have been talking about for sets of words from specific texts. We have framed this project in terms of professional development because that is what we think experiences creating this kind of instruction provide. Let us explain that a bit further by describing some ideas in the current thinking about professional development and how our approach fits into that.

Within the education field in general, there seems to be a consensus about principles of professional development that make those experiences effective. (See, e.g., Darling-Hammond & Cobb, 1996; Dole & Osborn, 2004; Elmore, 2002; Strickland, Kamil, Walberg, & Manning, 2004.) These principles include:

- building an understanding about the content of instruction
- providing sequential presentation of content
- offering models and examples of instruction as well as opportunities for teachers to produce their own examples
- providing feedback on developed examples and discussion over time
- ensuring that professional development experiences take place around actual teaching and learning interactions in classrooms

Our efforts toward promoting professional development for robust vocabulary instruction very much align with the principles above. We work with teachers to develop their ability to select Tier Two words—with mileage—from texts they use in their classrooms, to develop rich effective ways to introduce their meanings, and to follow up in order to provide multiple encounters and practice in actively using the words. Key to our thinking about providing professional development for robust vocabulary is that these experiences comprise both professional development and curriculum development. By that we mean that working through the development of instructional activities should provide a better understanding of robust vocabulary and how to develop the kinds of activities that bring it to life, and at the same time produce actual materials that can be used in the classroom.

Toward providing professional development—which in this instance means providing resources that allow teachers to engage in developing the steps of robust instruction—in this chapter we offer text selections that range from a read-aloud to a high school text that can be used as kind of exercises for engaging in the steps.

We see the material that follows as being used in one of two ways. First, it can be used in a collaborative group, perhaps at grade-level meetings or other inservice professional development gatherings. Second, we also expect that individual teachers and other readers may work through the materials on their own.

No matter whether you are working with a group or by yourself, we think the following pages will be most useful if you *engage* in each step of the planning process as we present it, then *compare* your decisions with our decisions, and finally *consider and reflect* on your initial decisions and choices and those that we suggest.

By way of initially engaging, we will always ask that you read a selection all the way through since we want to emphasize that robust vocabulary instruction does not start until after a story has been wrapped up, often through a discussion. A story is not merely a vessel for words. The story's ideas, events, descriptions, morals, and the like are the primary reasons for reading and thinking about it. The use of an author's words for extensive vocabulary development comes only after comprehension and interpretation has been well dealt with.

In the following sections, we provide texts and tasks for four grade spans: K–grade 3, grades 4–5, grades 6–8, and grades 9–12. We have found that teachers appreciate working with materials that relate to the grade level at which they teach. However, for more practice you may want to engage with more than one text and its tasks. For the most part, the only difference across the four grade spans is the complexity of the texts and the extent to which attention to text ideas is embedded within the instruction. As we mentioned in Chapter 4, attention to vocabulary tends to involve text ideas to a greater extent in the upper grades.

Each section begins with the grade-level specific text to read, followed by a sequence of activities for:

- selecting Tier Two words
- contextualizing the words based on their use in the text
- crafting student-friendly explanations for the words
- creating contexts for using the words that go beyond the text
- developing follow-up activities—we include a Menu of Instructional Activities (see Appendix A)
- constructing assessments

WORKING WITH A TEXT APPROPRIATE FOR STUDENTS IN KINDERGARTEN–GRADE 3

For developing vocabulary instruction for primary grades students, we use a short folktale, *The Tailor*, which can be used as a read-aloud for kindergarten and first-grade students or as a story that late second- and third-grade students read on their own.

Selecting Tier Two Words

Engage

Read the story and mark any Tier Two words that you think are candidates for after-reading robust instruction. We begin by mentioning that this short story has few Tier Two words from which to choose. But we managed to identify four candidates.

The Tailor

A folk tale retold by Ronette Killcrece Blake

Once upon a time, many, many years ago, there lived a poor, clever tailor. The tailor made beautiful clothing for all the townspeople. He worked hard every day, and lived quite simply. He was very frugal and never bought cloth to make something for himself.

One morning as he was unlocking his tailor shop door he saw a brown paper sack sitting at his stoop, with a small card attached. "This is for you," the note said. "Sincerely, A dear friend"

"Who could have left this?" the old man whispered to himself. He took the sack in between his wrinkled hands, and carefully untied the white string keeping the paper together. The tailor could not believe what he saw. A fine piece of red and gold cloth fell out. "What a fine piece of cloth!" he shouted. "I can't believe that someone would give me this beautiful cloth. I will make a fine coat out of this."

He measured, he figured, he cut, and he sewed. When he was done, he had a splendid new coat. He loved his coat very much, so he wore it every day. Through wind, and rain, and snow, and sleet, he wore his splendid coat. He wore it so much, that it was soon worn out.

Actually, it was not exactly all worn out. The tailor examined the coat carefully and saw that there were a few pieces that were not worn out. "This is still a fine piece of cloth!" he said. "I will make a fine pair of pants out of this." He measured, he figured, he cut, and he sewed. When he was done he had a splendid new pair of pants. He loved these pants very much, so he wore them every day. Through wind, and rain, and snow, and sleet, he wore these splendid pants. He wore them so much, that they were soon worn out.

Actually, they were not exactly all worn out. The tailor examined the pants carefully, and saw that there were a few pieces that were not worn out. "This is still a fine piece of cloth! I will make a fine hat out of this." He measured, he figured, he cut, and he sewed. When he was done he had a splendid new hat. He loved this hat very much, so he wore it every day. Through wind, and rain, and snow, and sleet, he wore this splendid hat. He wore it so much, that it was soon worn out.

Actually, it was not exactly all worn out. The tailor examined the hat carefully, and saw that there were a few pieces that were not worn out. "This is still a fine piece of cloth!" he said. "I will make a fine button out of this." He measured, he figured, he cut, and he sewed. When he was done he had a splendid new button. He loved this button very much, so he wore it every day. Through wind, and rain, and snow, and sleet, he wore his splendid button. He wore it so much, that it was soon worn out.

The tailor looked at the button, and he saw that the fine button was completely worn out. What was he to do?

He was a very clever tailor. So he made the button into . . . a story! It was a splendid story. He told it every day. And the story never, ever, wore out.

Compare

What words did you select? We identified *clever, frugal, splendid,* and *examined.*

Consider and Reflect

Another word we imagine you might have selected is *exclaimed.* We thought about selecting it too, but decided that it is heard so often in literature that it probably is implicitly understood. On the other hand, precisely because it is found in literature and we can imagine children using it in their writing, if it were directly dealt with, it might be a good word to use. The options then are to include *exclaimed,* exclude *exclaimed,* or exchange it for one of the other four words. Thinking about these options is quite useful because it raises issues about what is important in relation to what can get done.

Perhaps you considered the words *fine* and *measured.* We think that most primary-grade students have heard *fine* rather often and at least associate it with something positive. They well may not know that a characteristic of a "fine piece of cloth" may be delicacy. But that kind of enlargement of the basic idea that something that is *fine* is positive will occur over time without attention being brought to it. In the case of *measured,* again young children know that *measure* has something to do with size. The details of measurement will be a focus in mathematics.

So that we can all go ahead on the same page, so to speak, let's assume that we will work with the words *clever, frugal, splendid,* and *examined* from the text. Although four words is a reasonable number of words to target for robust instruction for young children, it is also the case that we have evidence that four words is not an upper limit for young children (Beck & McKeown, 2007). Just for the sake of illustration, let's say that we want six words—so that makes us two words short. In this case, we move to identifying "words about the story," our notion about labeling events and ideas in a text with Tier Two words that are not in the story (see Chapter 4, p. 41).

Selecting Words about the Story

Engage

Try to come up with two other words that are not in the story but that describe some aspect of the story. *The Tailor* is a sparse story, but there's still enough content for which to develop some labels. For this story you might want to think of interesting words to describe the major event, the nature of the tailor, or the tailor's reaction to something. We find that sometimes when teachers try this at first they tend to simply look for a single word in the story and come up with a synonym for it rather than thinking more broadly about some story idea. Toward spurring thinking for identifying good words about a story, we offer the following hints:

- Think in terms of looking for a concept or something that happened in the story that could be labeled rather than looking for a synonym for a word in the story. For instance, the word *material,* which is a synonym for *cloth,* would not be the best choice as far as a good Tier Two word with mileage.
- To prompt thinking about something within the story that can be labeled with a Tier Two word, we've found it useful to think about categories such as:
  - traits of a character
  - reactions to events
  - mood or setting
  - characterization of an event
  - interaction of characters
  - consequences of an event

Compare

What words did you come up with? Two ideas that came to us were that the tailor works very hard all the time and that the cloth could be used for many purposes. Thus, the two words about the story that we chose were *industrious* and *versatile.*

Consider and Reflect

You might have considered using the word *mystery* to describe the part where the tailor finds the cloth, or *creative* to describe the tailor's ability to use the cloth. *Mystery* has potential, but we would hesitate to use it because it could take the children down a garden path thinking about who left the cloth, when the core of the story is the idea that a story lasts forever. We would not use *creative* as it is close to *clever.* The distinctions between the two might be brought in after students knew one of the words well.

By the way, we particularly like *industrious* as it reminded us of when we were observing a first-grade teacher who told her class that "Jerome," who was hard at work at his desk, "was being industrious." The word took hold, and the teacher reported that over the next few days children would ask her whether she thought they were industrious and would describe someone as being industrious. The teacher then asked them to find someone in their neighborhood who was being industrious. Many reported having seen industrious people paving a street.

As for *versatile,* the multiple uses of the cloth allows its use. *Versatile* is a word with breadth of utility: there can be versatile things and versatile people.

So that all of us can stay together, we will use *clever, frugal, splendid, examined, industrious,* and *versatile* as our target words, acknowledging that someone else might have a somewhat different set.

Introducing the Words

Robust vocabulary instruction can be divided into two stages: Introduction and Follow-up. The Introduction occurs immediately after the selection has been read. The Follow-up occurs on subsequent days. First, we will deal with each of the components in our Introductions, which include the features noted in earlier sections and repeated below. We will ask you to engage in each introductory component.

- contextualizing the word
- providing a student-friendly explanation
- presenting alternative contexts for the word
- inviting students to interact with the word in a meaningful way

Contextualizing the Words Based on Their Use in the Text

Engage

Contextualize each word, that is, describe how each word or concept (for the words about the story) is used in the story.

Compare

Compare your sentences with ours.

- In the story, the tailor was described as *clever.*
- The tailor was also very *frugal* and never bought cloth to make something for himself.

- The first time the tailor used the cloth he made a *splendid* coat.
- Each time a piece of clothing wore out, the tailor *examined* it very carefully.
- The tailor worked very, very hard. Another way of saying that is that the tailor was *industrious*.
- In the story, the cloth the tailor used was good for making different things: a coat, pants, a hat, and then a button. Another way to say this is that the cloth was *versatile*.

Consider and Reflect

Since the words come from or are about a particular story, contextualizing the words is a pretty straightforward step. The only point that may vary is the extent to which you use the exact wording of the story. You may want to alter the wording to make it more conversational or to focus more squarely on the target word. As can be seen above, we have done it several ways. We think it's a good idea to change the wording within a set of target words so the context isn't presented in a formulaic way.

Crafting Student-Friendly Explanations

Engage

Develop a student-friendly explanation for each word.

Compare

Compare your friendly explanations with ours.

- Someone who is *clever* is good at figuring things out and solving problems.
- Someone who is *frugal* spends money very carefully and buys only what is necessary.
- Something *splendid* is wonderful, beautiful, and very special.
- If you *examine* something, you look at it very closely and carefully.
- Someone who is *industrious* works very hard and gets a lot done.
- If something is *versatile,* it can be used for many different things. People can be *versatile* too—a *versatile* person is able to do many different things well and can switch from one to the other quickly.

Consider and Reflect

As we have discussed in *Bringing Words to Life* and elsewhere in this volume (Chapter 3, p. 23), we have adopted a specific style for presenting word meanings that we call "student-friendly explanations." The easiest way to develop friendly explanations is to use the *COBUILD Dictionary,* making any adjustments as needed for the language level of the students or the particular sense that you want to focus on. In the table below, we explain some of the adjustments we made to some of the *COBUILD* definitions. The *Longman Dictionary* often has wording that is useful, although the style of definition is not that of a friendly explanation. If you do not have a *COBUILD* available, friendly explanations can be developed by working with traditional dictionary definitions and transforming the language. To aid the thinking process involved in developing friendly explanations, below we present the definitions from four dictionaries for the six *Tailor* story words.

| Word | Source of definition | | | |
	The American Heritage Dictionary of the English Language (Pickett et al., 2000)	*Word Central: Merriam– Webster Student's Electronic Dictionary* (2007)	*Longman Advanced American Dictionary* (Delacroix et al., 2007)	*Collins COBUILD Dictionary: English Language* (Sinclair et al., 1987)
clever	mentally quick and original	quick in learning	able to learn and understand things quickly	Someone who is clever is intelligent and able to learn and understand things easily.
frugal	practicing or marked by economy, as in the expenditure of money or the use of material resources	careful in spending or using resources	careful to buy only what is necessary	People who are frugal do not eat much or spend much money on themselves.
splendid	imposing by reason or showiness or grandeur; magnificent	impressive in beauty, grandeur, or excellence	excellent or very fine; beautiful and impressive	Something that is splendid is excellent and of very good quality, or is beautiful and impressive.
examined	to observe carefully or critically; inspect	to look at or check carefully	to look at, consider, or study something in order to find out about it	If you examine something, you look at it carefully or closely.

	Source of definition			
Word	*The American Heritage Dictionary of the English Language* (Pickett et al., 2000)	*Word Central: Merriam–Webster Student's Electronic Dictionary* (2007)	*Longman Advanced American Dictionary* (Delacroix et al., 2007)	*Collins COBUILD Dictionary: English Language* (Sinclair et al., 1987)
industrious	assiduous in work or study; diligent	constantly or regularly active or occupied	someone who is industrious tends to work hard	Someone who is industrious works very hard.
versatile	having varied uses or serving many functions	able to do many different kinds of things	having many different uses	Something such as a tool, machine, or material that is versatile can be used for many different purposes.

In the table below we explain the adjustments we made to some of the *COBUILD* definitions.

COBUILD definition	Our definition	Our explanation
Someone who is clever is intelligent and able to learn and understand things easily.	Someone who is clever is good at figuring things out and solving problems.	We didn't want to get learning and intelligence into it at this time. And given that the word is used to describe the tailor, he figured things out and solved problems.
People who are frugal do not eat much or spend much money on themselves.	Someone who is frugal spends money very carefully and buys only what is necessary.	We thought the focus on not eating much and not spending on themselves is a questionable focus for frugal. So we initiated the idea of not spending money and used the *Longman* idea of buying only what is needed.
Something that is splendid is excellent and of very good quality, or beautiful and impressive.	Something splendid is wonderful, beautiful, and very special.	We adopted the *COBUILD* features, but used words that are known to young children.
		(cont.)

COBUILD definition	Our definition	Our explanation
If you examine something, you look carefully or closely.	If you examine something you look at it very closely and carefully.	We used the *COBUILD* definition but included the pronoun *it* to reinforce that something is being looked at.
Someone who is industrious works very hard.	Someone who is industrious works very hard and gets a lot done.	We added the notion of "getting a lot done" because we tend to think that being industrious implies not only effort but also accomplishing things.
Something such as a tool, machine, or material that is versatile can be used for many different purposes.	If something is versatile, it can be used for many different things. People can be versatile too—a versatile person is able to do many different things well and can switch from one to the other quickly.	We preferred not specifically identifying examples of things (e.g., machines) that are versatile because children might get to the idea of everyday things, like a pot lid, being versatile. We included the idea of people being versatile as we had in mind that it would broaden our ability to develop subsequent materials.

Creating Contexts for Using the Words That Go Beyond the Text

Engage

Contextualize each word in a different way—that is, provide a sentence that shows how each word can be used in a context or situation that is not the same as the one in the story.

Compare

Compare your new contexts with ours.

- If you kept losing the key to your house, and decided to wear it on a chain around your neck—that would be a *clever* idea.
- It would be *frugal* to only buy clothes when there is a big sale.
- If you look out and see beautiful sunshine, you might think "What a *splendid* day!"
- If someone thought he or she might have found a ring with a real diamond in it, he or she would *examine* it very carefully.

- If someone cleaned a whole apartment building in one day, that would be *industrious*!
- Someone who can play the piano, drums, and trombone is a *versatile* musician.

Consider and Reflect

The importance of an additional context should not be underestimated because it is often the case that people limit the use of a new word to the context in which they first encountered it. (See also Chapter 3, p. 26.) Thus, we always provide at least one additional context for each word in the Introduction portion of robust instruction. Do your additional contexts provide features of the word not included in the original story context? Do the contexts provide other facets of how the words might be used?

Developing an Activity for Students to Interact with Word Meanings

The final step of the Introduction is to provide an opportunity for students to *interact* with the word. To this point, the teacher has presented information to the students: contextualized the word, provided a friendly explanation, and provided an additional context. Thus, the students have only listened. So, in the introductory phase for each word, the last step is an activity in which students *do* something to actively engage with the word's meaning. If students don't *do* something, it is questionable whether much learning can occur.

Engage

Develop a short activity that requires students to interact with each word's meaning. Since this should be a quick activity, it is best not to require any writing. You might want to consult the Menu of Instructional Activities in Appendix A as well as some examples in Chapter 6.

Compare

Say "Clever" if I describe something or someone who is clever. Say "No" if it is not clever. Students should be asked why they responded as they did.

- someone who figures out a shortcut for doing a math problem
- a pet who keeps trying to get out of its cage by chewing on the bars
- a baby who cries when he is hungry
- a student who uses new vocabulary words in her writing
- someone like the troll in *Three Billy Goats Gruff* who is fooled into letting the first two billy goats go across the bridge

Consider and Reflect

We think that a quick example/nonexample of a situation that could or could not be described as *clever* works well in this step of the Introduction. There are a couple things to keep in mind to make this format most effective: base the content of the examples on experiences, places, and characters that children are familiar with, and always ask "Why?" so that thinking about the word and its uses is made public.

Putting the Introduction to *clever* Together

Having discussed and asked you to engage in each of the steps in our Introduction phase one at a time, let's pause here and put all the parts together for the word *clever* as a way of illustrating how one word would be presented in a lesson.

clever

- *Contextualize*—In the story, the tailor was described as *clever.*
- *Friendly Explanation*—Someone who is *clever* is good at figuring things out and solving problems.
- *Additional Context*—If you kept losing the key to your house and decided to wear it on a chain around your neck—that would be a *clever* idea.

  Students engage with the word's meaning—Say "Clever" if I describe something or someone who is clever. Say "No" if it is not clever. Students should be asked why they responded as they did.

- Someone who figures out a shortcut for doing a math problem
- A pet who keeps trying to get out of its cage by chewing on the bars
- A baby who cries when he is hungry
- A student who uses new vocabulary words in her writing
- Someone like the troll in *Three Billy Goats Gruff* who is fooled into letting the first two billy goats go across the bridge

Follow-Up Interactions with the Words

After the words have been introduced, students need to interact with the words and their meanings on subsequent days. Recall that the goal of working with newly introduced words over several days is to keep new words in action for a while and, relatedly, to provide for frequent encounters. Additionally, continuing with newly introduced words for several days allows for enlarging the contexts in which students use the words and for supporting more complex thinking and writing with the words.

In Appendix A, our Menu of Instructional Activities provides examples of the kinds of activities that we would develop after the Introduction. These activities would take place across a week of instruction. Each activity should take about 3 to 15 minutes per day for a six-word set, 5 to 20 minutes for an 8–10 word set, and 10 to 25 minutes for a 10–15 word set. Of course, these estimated times are affected by how much writing and small-group activities are included.

Developing Three Days of Follow-Up Activities

Engage

For each of the words in *The Tailor*, develop two activities for each of 3 days that will get students to interact with each word's meaning.

It can help to start off the development of activities with some brainstorming of the kinds of topics you might associate with the words or how you might have students talk about and relate to the words. Below we present some quick brainstorming about contexts and topics that might help in developing activities for the words from *The Tailor* story. As you can see, what we provide is not complete and systematic, but it's a start for your thinking. It's been our experience that such starts ignite thinking about the words. For example, when we are working together and one of us comes up with a good example, it seems to spur on the process and all of us begin to suggest ideas. So we offer the quick brainstorming below in that spirit.

We thought of contexts that might be helpful for developing activities around some of the words:

- *clever*: magician tricks, dog tricks, children's hiding places, ways to make things out of empty boxes.
- *frugal*: saving your money, buying only what's needed, writing on both sides of your paper, making sure you get the last drop out of a bottle of ketchup.
- *industrious*: Students can demonstrate and explain how they would do the following in an industrious way and in a nonindustrious way: cleaning up the classroom, finishing writing a paper, shoveling snow.
- *splendid*: Students can explain what the following things would look like if they were splendid or not splendid: shoes, a cake, a party, a field trip.

The brainstorming above in conjunction with your ideas and the Menu of Instructional Activities in Appendix A should serve as the grist for creating follow-up activities.

Compare

Look over the activity formats in the Menu that you used to develop your activities.

Consider and Reflect

As you look over your activities, consider:

- Are they sequenced from simpler to more complex—for example, beginning with ones that require briefer responses to contexts, and moving to students creating their own contexts, and possibly to writing?
- Do you provide various ways for students to work and respond—for example, orally, with gestures, working with the whole class, working in groups/pairs?
- Are the words used in a variety of contexts so students get a full, well-rounded perspective on each word's use?
- Do the contexts used in the activities draw on students' interests and experiences?
- Are the activities interesting and fun?

Developing an Assessment

Engage

Develop an assessment for each of the words *frugal, splendid, examined, industrious,* and *versatile.* Check the discussion of assessment in Chapter 3.

Compare

Compare your assessment items with examples provided in Chapter 6.

Consider and Reflect

- Do the assessment items that you developed allow students to demonstrate their understanding of the words?
- Do the items reflect what you want to know about students' understanding of the words?
- Have you provided items that focus on contexts in which the words can be used appropriately, as well as items that focus on the meanings of the words?

WORKING WITH A TEXT APPROPRIATE FOR STUDENTS IN GRADES 4–5

For developing vocabulary instruction for students in the upper elementary grades, we use *The Cat and the Parrot*, which is a takeoff on an Indian folktale.

Selecting Tier Two Words

Engage

Read the story and mark any Tier Two words that you think are candidates for after-reading robust instruction. We found that this story had a number of Tier Two words. In the course of reading, we noted 10. After reviewing them we decided to use eight.

The Cat and the Parrot

An Indian folk tale retold by Maria Almendarez Barron

An unlikely pair of companions, a gregarious cat and a fun-loving parrot, decided that they should spend more time together. So they decided to have dinner together every week. They would take turns, eating at Cat's one week and eating at Parrot's the next week. Each felt that this idea was both equitable and fun.

"Fabulous!" said Parrot.

"Marvelous!" Cat agreed, "Why don't we start at my house?" And so the friends put their plan into action.

Cat set out a feast of the foods he liked best. There was a big bowl of warm milk. Next to this was a fine selection of imported raw fishes. The platter of fish was liberally garnished with fresh catnip, and the green herbs had been tied in artful bundles and tucked between fins and under gills. And for the crowning glory of this feast, Cat had made his special delicacy: fried mice. Now these were not just ordinary field mice, drab brown and tasting of the dirt they scurried through. No, these mice had been smuggled out of the laboratory in town, and they came in lovely shades of pure white, satiny black, golden beige and silvery gray, each with its own unique flavor. Cat had fried these delicious mice to crisp, golden, perfection. Needless to say, Cat was extremely proud of this feast.

When Parrot arrived at the door, Cat gave him a warm welcome, and announced that he had prepared the most delightful feast imaginable for his best friend.

"I have spared no expense, and every penny was worth it, for you dear friend!" Cat said as he threw open the door to the dining room.

Parrot looked at the spread of food in front of him. He looked at the seasoned fish, and the fried mice. His stomach turned as he realized that this feast was very different from the birdseed feasts that he was accustomed to. Parrot opened and closed his beak several times, but no words came out.

"I see that you are speechless," said Cat. "It is truly a fine sight to behold, isn't it?"

Parrot nodded weakly. He loved his good friend, and he didn't want to insult him by telling him that the spread in front of him was not his idea of good food. What should he do? What should he say? How could he get out of this without hurting Cat's feelings? Could he think of a plausible excuse?

Maybe he could say that he had strict orders from his doctor to limit his diet? Maybe he could tell Cat that his mother was unexpectedly visiting and he had to rush off to the airport? Maybe Cat would believe that he had developed a food allergy? No, he could not bear to tell such elaborate lies to his best friend.

Sweat gathered on Parrot's neck and trickled down his back. He was growing more and more desperate as he pondered a way to get out of staying for dinner.

"I am so sorry to confess this, dear Cat. I really didn't want to do anything that could disturb our perfect friendship, so I didn't mention this earlier. I honestly thought it might not be a problem. Well, in short . . . I . . . um . . . "

"Well spit it out!" Cat muttered, sounding slightly irritated.

Parrot could not lie to Cat but he could not bear to be completely honest and hurt Cat's feelings.

"I'm very sorry, Cat. Something has come up and I won't be able to stay for dinner after all," replied Parrot. He quickly gathered his belongings and with a swoop of his wings, he left Cat's home.

"I will have you over for dinner very soon to make up for this disturbance," Parrot called out as he swiftly flew toward home. "I feel just awful about disappointing you," he yelled with a dramatic sigh. And then he was out of sight.

Cat was indeed crestfallen and perplexed. All this delicious food! All his hard work! To say nothing of the expense! And Parrot left without much explanation! Now what was he to do? Fried mice certainly wouldn't keep. Perhaps he could freeze the fish for a chowder, but it was shameful to waste the gourmet fish on a soup. He heaved a sigh of his own, admitting defeat. Better to do as Parrot suggested than to try to force a meal on his poor friend.

One week later, Parrot welcomed Cat to a feast. "At least I have prepared a sensible feast," he thought to himself. "Food that really appeals to the gourmet."

"Thank you again for postponing our first dinner," Parrot said to Cat. "I have quite a meal planned. In fact . . . "

With a flourish Parrot opened his dining room door.

Cat looked at the overflowing table. "I . . . I . . . I . . . um, well . . . you see . . . " sputtered Cat.

Prodigious mounds of hard, dried seeds were spread in front of him. A tray of juicy, ripe fruit separated each type of seed from its neighbor. The overpoweringly sweet aroma hung like a cloud above the dining room table.

"That is to say . . . I mean . . . " Cat ground to a halt, and hung his head. "Is this really what you eat every day?"

"Oh heavens no!" replied Parrot. "I had to special order five of these seeds from Madagascar—I would never indulge like this when alone! And don't even get me started on how hard I worked to age these fruits to perfection. Each peach, every mango, and the entire tower of bananas has been ripened until each is bursting from its skin. Just oozing all that delectable juice! It took me the entire week to prepare. But, my understanding friend, I could do no less to repay you for your generosity and my abrupt departure last week!"

"Well this is indeed a fine effort," Cat responded, as he ground his toe into the carpet. He didn't look at Parrot. Instead he busily picked at a thread on his coat.

"You don't look very excited about my feast! Frankly, I expected a little more enthusiasm," said Parrot, feeling disheartened.

"Let's sit down," Cat said. "I feel dreadfully embarrassed, but I think we better talk about this plan of ours. You see, I don't like fruit any more than you apparently like fried mice! We each went to a lot of trouble, but never talked to each other about it until it was too late!"

With that, the two friends started laughing, and they sat down to rethink their plan.

Compare

Which words did you choose? We chose *gregarious, equitable, plausible, elaborate, perplexed, prodigious, abrupt,* and *disheartened.*

Consider and Reflect

Of the words above, we were particularly taken with *gregarious, plausible, perplexed,* and *prodigious.* There are several reasons we liked *gregarious,* but in particular we can see it incorporated into intermediate-grade students' experiences to the extent that they talk about friendly people and outgoing people. *Plausible* is a fairly sophisticated word and captures so well the kind of complicated concept of something "seeming to be right." *Perplexed* is a reasonable alternative for "I'm confused," which certainly is used by fourth and fifth graders. *Prodigious* is a literary word and probably new to most intermediate students. It can range broadly from size, to capacity, to activity (one could eat prodigiously). As for *equitable, abrupt,* and *disheartened,* we thought *equitable* was a good alternative for "That's not fair!" and *abrupt* a good alternative for *suddenly,* while *disheartened* is a way to describe feelings that students may have had.

Two other words that we considered but did not include were *garnished* and *delectable.* We decided not to include *garnished* as its typical use is most often only narrowly associated with food, although it can be applied more broadly. Our decision not to use it is that the other words seemed more valuable. However, an argument could be made to use *garnished.* We excluded *delectable* as it is such a near synonym of *delicious* and *scrumptious* that its availability to a learner may not be so valuable. But there is nothing absolute about those decisions, and some of you might well decide to include those words.

Thinking about which words to include is quite useful beyond making a decision about, say, whether to include a specific word like *garnished.* The usefulness of thinking about such decision is in the "thought." "Should I include *X* or *Y*? Would it take too much time to include both? If time is such that I can include just one, which will be more useful . . . interesting?" are examples of the kind of reflection that is characteristic of teachers' problem solving and decision making.

Selecting Words about the Story

As we've seen above, *The Cat and the Parrot* has a number of good Tier Two words—in fact, more than we discussed (e.g., *crestfallen, delicacy*). It is the case, however, that sometimes good texts do not include as many Tier Two words as a teacher might like for, say, a week of vocabulary work. In such cases, we have talked about identifying words *about* the story (see Chapter 4, pp. 41 and 42). Even when there are enough words in a text for a generous set to work with, a reason to include a word or two that are not in the story is that it or they capture a theme or major event. This was the case for the word *perspective*. When we read *The Cat and the Parrot*, *perspective* came to mind because the major point of the story is that both animals viewed food that they liked from their own *perspective*. *Perspective* is a great Tier Two word and can range broadly, so even though there are enough good words within the story, we would include *perspective*.

Engage

Although it is not necessary for this story, we thought that it was a good idea to bring up the issue of identifying words *about* the story up for consideration as a professional development exercise. So we ask you to come up with a word or two that is not in the story, but that captures an event or general understanding that is in the story. We find that sometimes when teachers try this, they tend to come up with a synonym for an existing word from the story rather than thinking more broadly about some story idea. Toward spurring thinking for identifying good words *about* a story, we offer the following hints.

- Think in terms of looking for a concept or something that happened in the story that could be labeled rather than looking for a synonym for a word in the story. For instance, the word *scrumptious,* which is a synonym for *delectable,* would not be the best choice as far as a good Tier Two word with mileage as it is just a near synonym for *delectable.*
- To prompt thinking about something within the story that can be labeled with a Tier Two word, we've found it useful to think about categories such as:
  - traits of a character
  - reactions to events
  - mood or setting
  - characterization of an event
  - interaction of characters
  - consequences of an event

Compare

What words did you come up with? Two ideas that came to us were that both characters wanted to be *hospitable* and that Parrot found himself in a *predicament* when the food Cat had prepared was uneatable, and yet he didn't want to hurt Cat's feelings.

Consider and Reflect

Being able to incorporate words that are not in the story—either because there are not enough Tier Two words in a given text or there is a word that characterizes the theme, such as our choice of *perspective*—enlarges the teacher's opportunities for targeting good words. But at first some teachers have difficulty. Hence, we will use our list of categories vis-à-vis *The Cat and the Parrot*, and see what we can come up with.

- Traits of a character—*Hospitable* and *gracious* came to mind when we thought about character traits.
- Reactions to events—*Predicament* was targeted by our thinking of Parrot's reaction to the food and his concern for not being rude to Cat.
- Mood or setting—This category did not help us trigger any words.
- Characterization of an event—We thought about labeling the dinners as *catastrophes*.
- Interaction of characters—*Sociable* or perhaps *affable* seemed to be appropriate words.
- Consequences of an event—At the end, the characters were *forthright* or *candid* with one another.

Our final set will include the nine words from the story: *gregarious, equitable, plausible, elaborate, perplexed, prodigious, abrupt, disheartened,* and *perspective.* It is important to point out that this is not the *only* set of words for *The Cat and the Parrot*. It is a good set of Tier Two words that was identified by thinking of which words had mileage and whether any words about the story should be included. Sets other people develop from this story would probably have many similarities to ours, but also some differences.

Introducing the Words

Robust vocabulary instruction can be divided into two stages: Introduction and Follow-up. The Introduction occurs immediately after the selection has been read. The Follow-up occurs on subsequent days. First, we will ask you to develop each of the components in our Introductions, which include the features noted in earlier sections and repeated below.

- contextualizing the word
- providing a student-friendly explanation
- presenting alternative contexts for the word
- inviting students to interact with the word in a meaningful way

Contextualizing the Words Based on Their Use in the Text

Engage

Contextualize each word—that is, describe how each word or concept (for the words about the story) is used in the story.

- The cat in the story was described as *gregarious*.
- In the story, Cat and Parrot thought that taking turns eating at each others' house would be an *equitable* plan.
- Parrot was trying to think of a *plausible* excuse about not eating Cat's food.
- Parrot thought that it would be an *elaborate* lie to tell Cat that he had developed a food allergy.
- Cat was *perplexed* when Parrot left without eating dinner.
- Parrot had prepared *prodigious* mounds of seeds for dinner with Cat.
- In the story, Parrot wanted to repay Cat for the *abrupt* way he had left Cat's house.
- Parrot felt *disheartened* at Cat's lack of enthusiasm for the dinner he had prepared.
- Cat and Parrot both prepared dinner based on their *perspective* about what food was most delicious.

Compare

Compare your additional contexts with ours.

Consider and Reflect

Since the words come from or are about a particular story, contextualizing the words is a pretty straightforward step. The only point that may vary is the extent to which you use the exact wording of the story. You may want to alter the wording to make it more conversational or to focus more squarely on the target word. As can be seen above, we have done it several ways. We think it's a good idea to change the wording within a set so the context isn't presented in a formulaic way.

Crafting Student-Friendly Explanations

Engage

Develop a student-friendly explanation for each word.

Compare

Compare your friendly explanations with ours.

- Someone who is *gregarious* enjoys being with other people.
- Something that is *equitable* is fair, with everyone being treated equally.
- Something that is *plausible* is reasonable and probably true.
- If something is *elaborate*, then it is planned with a lot of attention given to all the details.

- Someone who is *perplexed* is confused and maybe a little worried.
- Something that is *prodigious* is so large that it might amaze people.
- If something happens that is *abrupt,* it is very sudden and not expected.
- If you are *disheartened,* you feel disappointed about something and have less hope about it than you did before.
- Someone's *perspective* is *his or her* way of thinking about something.

Consider and Reflect

As we have discussed in *Bringing Words to Life* and elsewhere in this volume (Chapter 3, p. 23), we have adopted a specific style for presenting word meanings that we call "student-friendly explanations." The easiest way to develop friendly explanations is to use the *COBUILD Dictionary,* making any adjustments as needed for the language level of the students or the specific sense that you want to focus on. The *Longman Dictionary* often has wording that is useful, although the style of definition is not that of a friendly explanation. If you do not have a *COBUILD* or *Longman* available, friendly explanations can be developed by working with traditional dictionary definitions and transforming the language. To aid the thinking process involved in developing friendly explanations, below we present the definitions from four dictionaries for the nine *The Cat and the Parrot* story words.

	Source of definition			
Word	*The American Heritage Dictionary of the English Language* (Pickett et al., 2000)	*Word Central: Merriam–Webster Student's Electronic Dictionary* (2007)	*Longman Advanced American Dictionary* (Delacroix et al., 2007)	*Collins COBUILD Dictionary: English Language* (Sinclair et al., 1987)
gregarious	seeking and enjoying the company of others; sociable	marked by a liking for companionship	Someone who is gregarious is friendly and enjoys being with other people.	Someone who is gregarious enjoys being with other people.
equitable	marked by or having equity; just and impartial	being fair or just	fair and equal to everyone involved	Something that is equitable is fair and reasonable in a way that gives equal treatment to everyone.

(cont.)

	Source of definition			
Word	*The American Heritage Dictionary of the English Language* (Pickett et al., 2000)	*Word Central: Merriam–Webster Student's Electronic Dictionary* (2007)	*Longman Advanced American Dictionary* (Delacroix et al., 2007)	*Collins COBUILD Dictionary: English Language* (Sinclair et al., 1987)
plausible	seemingly valid, likely, or acceptable; credible	appearing worthy of belief	a statement that is plausible is reasonable and seems likely to be true	A plausible explanation, argument, or statement is one that seems likely to be true or valid.
elaborate	intricate and rich in detail	made or done with great care or with much detail	carefully planned and produced with many details	Elaborate plans, methods, etc., are carefully planned or organized with great attention to detail.
perplexed	filled with confusion or bewilderment; puzzled	to make difficult to understand	confused and worried by something that you cannot understand	To perplex someone means to cause him to feel confused and slightly worried because he does not completely understand.
prodigious	impressively great in size, force or extent; enormous	very big: huge	extremely or surprisingly large or powerful	Something that is prodigious is so large in size or in amount that it causes amazement.
abrupt	unexpectedly sudden	sudden, rudely brief	sudden and unexpected	If an action, change, or ending is abrupt, it is sudden and perhaps surprising or unpleasant.
disheartened	to shake or destroy the courage or resolution of; dispirit	to deprive of courage and hope	disappointed, so that you lose hope and do not feel determined to continue doing something anymore	If you are disheartened, you feel disappointed about something and have less confidence or less hope about it than you did before.

Word	Source of definition			
	The American Heritage Dictionary of the English Language (Pickett et al., 2000)	*Word Central: Merriam–Webster Student's Electronic Dictionary* (2007)	*Longman Advanced American Dictionary* (Delacroix et al., 2007)	*Collins COBUILD Dictionary: English Language* (Sinclair et al., 1987)
perspective	a mental view or outlook	point of view	a way of thinking about something, which is influenced by the kind of person you are or by your experiences	A perspective is a particular way of thinking about or viewing something, especially one that is influenced by your beliefs or experiences.

In the table below we explain the adjustments we made to some of the *COBUILD* definitions.

COBUILD definition	Our definition	Our explanation
Someone who is *gregarious* enjoys being with other people.	Someone who is gregarious enjoys being with other people.	We used the *COBUILD* definition.
Something that is *equitable* is fair and reasonable in a way that gives equal treatment to everyone.	Something that is equitable is fair with everyone being treated equally.	We omitted the idea of reasonable, and changed the statement "that gives equal treatment to everyone" to "everyone being treated equally."
A *plausible* explanation, argument, or statement is one that seems likely to be true or valid.	Something that is plausible is reasonable and probably true.	We substituted simpler words (e.g., *true* for *valid*) and omitted some words (e.g., *argument, statement*).
Elaborate plans, methods, etc., are carefully planned or organized with great attention to detail.	If something is elaborate, it is planned with a lot of attention given to all the details.	We chose not to include specific examples of things and used a simpler sentence structure. *(cont.)*

COBUILD definition	Our definition	Our explanation
To *perplex* someone means to cause them to feel confused and slightly worried because they do not completely understand.	Someone who is *perplexed* is confused and maybe a little worried.	We simplified the language.
Something that is *prodigious* is so large in size or in amount that it causes amazement.	Something that is *prodigious* is so large that it might amaze people.	We simplified the language.

Creating Contexts for Using the Words That Go Beyond the Text

Engage

Decontextualize each word—that is, provide a sentence that shows how each word can be used in a context or situation that is not the same as the one in the story.

Compare

Compare your new contexts with ours.

- Someone who is *gregarious* would talk with other people when he rode a bus.
- It would be *equitable* if there were eight people at dinner and your aunt cut a pie into perfect one-eighth pieces.
- It is *plausible* that school would be called off if 3 feet of snow fell overnight.
- The cake was *elaborately* decorated with many different colorful flowers.
- Because Sarah's mother told her she was forbidden to attend concerts, Sarah was *perplexed* when her mother handed her a ticket to see Gym Class Heroes.
- The scientist received a *prodigious* award for her work on global warming.
- The weather changed *abruptly* from sunny to rainy.
- The football team was *disheartened* after its 30-point loss to a mediocre team.
- From an infant's *perspective,* the English language may appear to be nothing but garbled sounds.

Consider and Reflect

The importance of an additional context should not be underestimated because it is not that uncommon for people to limit the use of a new word to the context in which they first encountered it (see Chapter 3, p. 26). Thus, we always provide at least one additional context for each word in the Introduction portion of robust vocabulary instruction. Do your additional contexts provide features of the word not included in the original story context? Does it provide another facet of how the word might be used?

Developing an Activity for Students to Interact with Word Meanings

The final step of the Introduction is to provide an opportunity for students to *interact* with the word. To this point, the teacher has presented information to the students: contextualized the word, provided a friendly explanation, and provided an additional context. Thus, the students have only listened. So, in the introductory phase for each word, the last step is an activity in which students do something to actively engage with the word's meaning. If students don't *do* something, it is questionable whether much learning can occur.

Engage

Develop a short activity that requires students to interact with each word's meaning. Since this should be a quick activity, it is best not to require any writing. You might want to consult the Menu of Instructional Activities in Appendix A as well as some examples in Chapter 6.

Compare

- Which would a *gregarious* person be likely to do, stay home and watch TV, or go plan a party for his friends. Why?
- Which would be more *elaborate,* a hat decorated with 50 little feathers or a hat decorated with a big feather? Why?
- What would be more *equitable,* having the entire class take turns cleaning the classroom, or making only the boys do the cleaning? Why?
- Which would be a more *plausible* excuse for not doing your homework—that your bird ate it or that you left your book in school? Why?
- What would cause you to be more *perplexed,* if it rained in December or if it snowed in July? Why?
- What would be a more *prodigious* event, the president's inaugural address or a Friday night football game? Why?
- If a car coasted slowly to its final destination, would that be an *abrupt* stop? Why?
- Would you be more *disheartened* if you lost your lunch or an expensive piece of jewelry? Why?
- If you walked down a deserted alley during the day and then again at night, would you have the same *perspective* of that alley? Why?

Consider and Reflect

We think that choosing between an example and a nonexample of a word works well in this step of the Introduction. A couple things to keep in mind to make this format most effective: base the content of the examples on experiences, places, and characters that students are familiar with, and always ask "Why?" so that thinking about the word and its uses is made public.

Putting the Introduction to *gregarious* Together

Having discussed and asked you to engage in each of the steps in our Introduction phase one at a time, let's pause here and put all the parts together for the word *gregarious* as a way of illustrating how it would be introduced in a lesson.

gregarious

- *Contextualize*—In the story, the cat was described as *gregarious.*
- *Friendly Explanation*—Someone who is *gregarious* is friendly and wants to be with other people.
- *Additional Context*—Someone who is *gregarious* would talk with other people when he rode on a bus.
- *Students engage with the word's meaning*—Say "Gregarious" if I describe someone who is gregarious. Say "No" if someone is not gregarious. Students should be asked why they responded as they did.
  - someone who can't wait to get to a party
  - someone who talks to everyone he meets
  - someone who loves to stay home and watch TV
  - someone who only goes to the movies with her friends
  - someone who would not get up early to go on a camping trip with the other kids in her neighborhood

Follow-Up Interactions with the Words

After the words have been introduced, students need to interact with the words and their meanings on subsequent days. Recall that the goal of working with newly introduced words over several days is to keep new words in action for a while and, relatedly, to provide for frequent encounters. Additionally, continuing with newly introduced words for several days allows for enlarging the contexts in which students use the words and for supporting more complex thinking and writing with the words.

In Appendix A, our Menu of Instructional Activities provides examples of the kinds of activities that we would develop for the week after the Introduction. Each activity should take about 3 to 15 minutes per day for a six-word set, 5 to 20 minutes for an 8–10 word set, and 10 to 25 minutes for a 10–15 word set. Of course, these estimated times are affected by how much writing and small-group activities are included.

Developing Three Days of Follow-Up Activities

Engage

For each of the words in *The Cat and the Parrot*, develop two activities for each of 3 days that will get students to interact with each word's meaning. It can help to start off the development of activities with some brainstorming of the kinds of topics you might associate with the words or how you might have students talk about and relate to the words. Below we present some quick brainstorming about contexts and topics that might help in developing activities for the words from *The Cat and the Parrot*. As you can see, what we provide is not complete and systematic, but it's a start for your thinking. It's been our experience that such starts ignite the thinking about the words. For example, when we are working together and one of us comes up with a good example, it seems to spur on the process and all of us begin to suggest ideas. So we offer the quick brainstorming below in that spirit.

- The word *perspectives* provides good opportunities for a compare/contrast activity—for example, how would an ant's and an elephant's perspectives differ about how *prodigious* a slice of cheese is.
- Students can explain how things could be *elaborate* and not elaborate: a story, party decorations, an excuse.
- Students can think about why they might be *perplexed* by their pet, their breakfast, and their teacher.
- Ask students to demonstrate how they would do the following *abruptly*: stop writing, turn around, stand up, sit down.
- Ask students to explain what might make the following feel *disheartened*: a teacher, a salesman, an astronaut.

The brainstorming above in conjunction with your ideas and the Menu of Instructional Activities in Appendix A should serve as the grist for creating follow-up activities.

Compare

Look over the activity formats in the Menu that you used to develop your activities.

Consider and Reflect

As you look over your activities, consider:

- Are they sequenced from simpler to more complex—for example, beginning with ones that require briefer responses to contexts and moving to students creating their own contexts, and possibly to writing?

- Do you provide various ways for students to work and respond—for example, orally, with gestures, working with the whole class, working in groups/pairs?
- Are the words used in a variety of contexts so students get a full, well-rounded perspective on each word's use?
- Do the contexts used in the activities draw on students' interests and experiences?
- Are the activities interesting and fun?

Developing an Assessment

Engage

Develop an assessment for each of the words *gregarious, equitable, plausible, elaborate, perplexed, prodigious, abrupt, disheartened,* and *perspective.* Check the discussion of assessment in Chapter 3.

Compare

Compare your assessment items with examples provided in Chapter 6.

Consider and Reflect

- Do the assessment items that you developed allow students to demonstrate their understanding of the words?
- Do the items reflect what you want to know about students' understanding of the words?
- Have you provided items that focus on contexts in which the words can be used appropriately, as well as items that focus on the meanings of the words?

WORKING WITH A TEXT APPROPRIATE FOR STUDENTS IN GRADES 6–8

For developing vocabulary instruction for middle school students, we use a brief tale called *The Bridge on the River Clarinette.* This story, though quite short, offers a good selection of Tier Two vocabulary, and many of the words are tied strongly to the theme of the story. Something we particularly like about this story is the role played by "the teacher." We think you'll agree!

Selecting Tier Two Words

Engage

Read the story and mark any Tier Two words that you think are candidates for after-reading robust instruction. We identified seven words from the story.

The Bridge on the River Clarinette

by Pierre Gamarra
Translated from the French by Paulette Henderson

The inhabitants of the little town of Framboisy-sur-Clarinette were worried. The bridge that spanned the River Clarinette was about to collapse. And if the bridge did collapse, the citizens of Framboisy would lose touch with the rest of France. There would be no more trade, no more traffic, no more tourists.

It was therefore necessary to reconstruct the bridge. But Framboisy was poor, and the town council was deeply troubled.

Just the other morning—on Framboisy's large central plaza—Monsieur Leopold, the owner of the Green Swan Inn, greeted Madame Barbette, the grocer. "How are things with you this morning, Madame Barbette?"

"Very bad, Monsieur Leopold. Business is falling off. I did not sell more than one package of macaroni last week. People just don't have money anymore."

Monsieur Leopold sighed. "As for me, I don't have customers either. The tourists don't dare cross the bridge nowadays."

"Did it split last night?"

"Yes, it did; I heard it. It's a disgrace. It could cave in at any moment."

"What's to become of us? What we need is a new bridge."

At that moment Monsieur Leopold and Madame Barbette saw the mayor and the teacher coming out of the town hall.

"Well, well, gentlemen," said Monsieur Leopold, "how are town matters going? Are we going to rebuild the bridge?"

The mayor shook his head with infinite sadness. "The council has examined various bridge plans. But it's an outrageously expensive undertaking. We'll never be able to pay for it."

"Nevertheless, you must make a decision," insisted Madame Barbette, nearly stabbing the mayor with her long, pointed nose. "Without a bridge we're ruined. No one dares to venture across our dilapidated old bridge."

The teacher shaded his eyes and gazed in the direction of the bridge. "Someone is coming!" he called.

"Stranger! Impossible! He wasn't afraid to cross," cried Monsieur Leopold.

"Amazing!" agreed the teacher. "But what an odd sort of person, all dressed in red and black and hopping from side to side. Look at his strange, uncanny smile, and the glint in his eyes."

The stranger approached the group and bowed to each of the citizens with great respect. His eyes glowed like deep red rubies. "I am very honored," he said, "to be visiting the distinguished inhabitants of Framboisy-sur-Clarinette."

"Monsieur is traveling?" the innkeeper asked politely.

"I'm going about the land on business."

"Monsieur is a businessman, then?" queried the teacher.

"Yes, I buy and I sell."

"And what is it that you sell?"

"Anything and everything."

"Anything and everything?"

"Yes, anything at all. Sausages, cars, houses, shirts, bridges . . . "

The mayor stepped forward. "Did you say bridges? You sell bridges?"

"But of course. Bridges. All sorts of bridges. Big ones, small ones, medium-sized ones. Made of wood, iron, even concrete."

The mayor scratched his head. "It just so happens that, at this time, we are in need of a bridge. A solid bridge with two or three arches."

"Easy!" said the stranger with a soft little laugh.

"And what is the price of a bridge?" demanded Madame Barbette defiantly.

"Nothing at all."

The four inhabitants of Framboisy jumped for joy, but the teacher said, "That can't be true. If you build us a new bridge, certainly you will ask us for something in exchange."

"Almost nothing," said the stranger.

"What would you ask of us?"

"Your words."

To the astonishment of his audience, the stranger explained, "You give me your words, and I will build you a beautiful bridge in five seconds. Note that I am not asking for *all* your words; I will leave you a few for your daily needs—*drink, eat, sleep, bread, butter, coffee* . . . "

"I don't understand," murmured the teacher. "What are you going to do with our words?"

"That's *my* business," said the stranger. "Promise that you will give me your words, and I will build you a bridge—a magnificent concrete and steel bridge, guaranteed for ten centuries!"

"It's a bad joke," muttered the mayor. "And furthermore, if you take our words, we shall find it very difficult to converse."

"No, no, no. I will leave you enough to satisfy you. Do you really have to talk so much? I'll leave you the most important words. And you shall have an extraordinary bridge in five seconds."

"So you're a magician, then?" asked the innkeeper.

"I have a very advanced technique at my disposal," the stranger replied modestly.

"We could at least give it a try," said Monsieur Leopold.

"All right," said Madame Barbette. "Let him have our words, and we shall have our bridge."

"I object!" cried the teacher. "We should never give up our words. At any rate, it's a crazy joke. Do you really think that a bridge can be built in five seconds?"

"Let us try, anyway," said the innkeeper.

"You agree, then?" concluded the stranger with a somewhat malicious swiftness. "I leave you a few words—as I said before: *bread, milk, eat, drink, sleep, house, chair*—and I build you an extraordinary bridge?"

"Agreed," said the mayor, the innkeeper, and the grocer.

The teacher shook his head in refusal. Too late. The stranger was already turning toward the dilapidated bridge, pointing his index finger. And all of a sudden there arose a beautiful three-arched bridge, silhouetted against the sky.

The mayor nudged the innkeeper and said, "Bread, butter, eat, drink."

The innkeeper looked at him and replied, "Drink, sleep, house, chair."

Compare

What words did you select? We identified *inhabitants, ruined, dilapidated, uncanny, distinguished, astonishment,* and *malicious.*

Consider and Reflect

There are several other possibilities that we imagine you may have considered. Others we initially noted are *glint, ventured, defiantly,* and *magnificent.* We easily decided against *glint* and *ventured,* as *glint* seems interesting but limited in its range, and *ventured* seems a bit hollow in terms of meaning—it kind of just means "went there"—and the story offers many stronger candidates. We like *defiantly,* but don't think it is used particularly strongly here—Mme. Barbette "defiantly" demands the price of the bridge, but she does not seem especially defiant. *Magnificent* is a good word, but basically just another synonym for *great, terrific,* and so on—so probably not that key to learn, and more likely to be picked up from contexts than many other words. We found some other Tier Two words in the story, but judged them as probably already known by middle schoolers: *gazed, murmured, muttered,* and *insist.* Of course, deciding these are familiar is a judgment call, and depends on knowing the vocabulary level of particular students.

As far as the words we did select, here is some of our thinking:

- *Inhabitants* defines the characters of the story, and the word has a rich morphological family: *habitat, habit, inhabit.* So we think it is worth teaching.
- *Dilapidated* is the state of the bridge that provides the central problem of the story—and it is a great word to say and makes for good images.
- *Uncanny* is the essence of the character of the stranger, and it has a strong, unique meaning.
- *Malicious* is the key to the motives of the stranger.
- *Distinguished* is used in such an interesting way in the story—the stranger says he is "honored ... to be visiting the distinguished inhabitants of Framboisy-sur-Clarinette." But given his later actions, he almost seems to be mocking them with this honorific.

Our other choices—*ruined* and *astonishment*—were selected just because we like them and they seem to round out the set of choices.

So let's assume that we will work with the words *inhabitants, ruined, dilapidated, uncanny, distinguished, astonishment,* and *malicious* from the text. Seven words is a rather small number of words to target for robust instruction for middle schoolers. Even though there are other story words we could have chosen, we have decided to move to adding "words about the story," our notion about labeling events and ideas in a text with Tier Two words that are not in the story (see Chapter 4, p. 41).

Selecting Words about the Story

Engage

Try to come up with two other words that are not in the story. *The Bridge on the River Clarinette* story offers a lot of possibilities because of the "Be careful what you wish for" nature of the unfolding events. We find that sometimes when teachers try to find words about the story, at first they tend to come up with a synonym for an existing word rather than thinking more broadly about some story *idea.* Toward spurring thinking for identifying good words about a story, we offer the following hints.

- Think in terms of looking for a concept or something that happened in the story that could be labeled rather than looking for a synonym for a word in the story. For instance, the word *variety,* which is a synonym for *all sorts* (of bridges), or *purchase* for *buy* would not be the strongest choices as far as good Tier Two words with mileage. Also, they are very much incidental in the story. Aiming for words about the story provides a good opportunity to think at more of a theme or interpretive level.
- To prompt thinking about something within the story that can be labeled with a Tier Two word, we've found it useful to think about categories such as:
  - traits of a character
  - reactions to events
  - mood or setting
  - characterization of an event
  - interaction of characters
  - consequences of an event

Compare

What words did you come up with? In this story, we think that character traits is an especially strong direction to go in. To our thinking, there are a couple of words that strongly fit the characters in this story and have a role in the story's outcome. They are *susceptible*—which is what most of the characters were to the stranger's offer— and *skeptical*—which is what the clear-thinking teacher (hooray for teachers!) was.

Consider and Reflect

Some other words that we thought of that fit the story were *compliant*, which describes how most of the characters reacted to the stranger; *isolated*, which is what the people in the town wanted to avoid being—but were indeed left rather isolated by their inability to communicate; and *regret*, which we imagine they may be feeling as the result of giving in to the stranger. Although these are all good words, we prefer *susceptible* and *skeptical* because we think they are strong useful words on their own, and they play off each other so well. You may have come up with others, as this story is rich in possibility.

Introducing the Words

Robust vocabulary instruction can be divided into two stages: Introduction and Follow-up. The Introduction occurs after the selection has been read. The Follow-up occurs on subsequent days. First, we will deal with each of the components in our Introductions, which include the features noted in earlier sections and repeated below. We will ask you to engage in each introductory component.

- contextualizing the word
- providing a student-friendly explanation
- presenting alternative contexts for the word
- inviting students to interact with the word in a meaningful way

Contextualizing the Words Based on Their Use in the Text

Engage

Contextualize each word—that is, provide a sentence that describes how each word or concept (for the words about the story) is used in the story.

Compare

Compare your sentences with ours.

- The story is about the *inhabitants* of a little town.
- The people were afraid that their town would be *ruined* if the bridge broke down.
- The bridge in the town was old and *dilapidated*.
- The odd stranger who came to town had an *uncanny* smile.
- The stranger said he was honored to visit the *distinguished* people of the town.
- The people expressed *astonishment* when the stranger said he could build a bridge in 5 seconds.

- The stranger seemed *malicious* when the townspeople agreed to let him build the bridge.
- The stranger's great offer easily influenced some of the people who eagerly agreed to let him build the bridge. Another way to say this is that the townspeople were *susceptible* to the stranger's offer.
- The teacher was not so sure about the stranger and his ways. Another way to capture that idea is to say that the teacher seemed *skeptical* of the strange visitor.

Consider and Reflect

Since the words come from or are about a particular story, contextualizing the words is a pretty straightforward step. The only point that may vary is the extent to which you use the exact wording of the story. You may want to alter the wording to make it more conversational or to focus more squarely on the target word. As can be seen above, we have done it several ways. We think it's a good idea to change the wording within a set of target words so the context isn't presented in a formulaic way.

Crafting Student-Friendly Explanations

Engage

Develop a student-friendly explanation for each word.

Compare

Compare your friendly explanations with ours.

- The *inhabitants* of a place are all the people who live there.
- If something is *ruined*, it has been destroyed and can't function or be used any longer.
- Something *dilapidated* is falling apart and almost completely broken down.
- If people or things are *uncanny*, they are surprising and strange in almost a scary way.
- People who are *distinguished* are highly respected and admired, usually for work they have done.
- If you express *astonishment*, you feel suddenly shocked and surprised.
- If someone does something *malicious*, he acts deliberately mean or evil.
- If you are *susceptible* to something, you are too easily influenced by it.
- If you are *skeptical* about something, you have some doubts about whether it is true or right.

Consider and Reflect

As we have discussed in *Bringing Words to Life* and elsewhere in this volume (see Chapter 3, p. 23), we have adopted a specific style for presenting word meanings that we call "student-friendly explanations." The easiest way to develop friendly explanations is to use the *COBUILD Dictionary,* making any adjustments as needed for the language level of the students or the specific sense that you want to focus on. If you do not have a *COBUILD* available, friendly explanations can be developed by working with traditional dictionary definitions and transforming the language. The *Longman Dictionary* often has wording that is useful, although the style of definition is not that of a friendly explanation. To aid the thinking process involved in developing friendly explanations, below we present the definitions from four dictionaries for the Tier Two words for *The Bridge on the River Clarinette.*

	Source of definition			
Word	*The American Heritage Dictionary of the English Language* (Pickett et al., 2000)	*Word Central: Merriam–Webster Student's Electronic Dictionary* (2007)	*Longman Advanced American Dictionary* (Delacroix et al., 2007)	*Collins COBUILD Dictionary: English Language* (Sinclair et al., 1987)
inhabitants	one that inhabits a place, especially as a permanent resident	one who lives permanently in a place	people who live in a particular place	The inhabitants of a place are the people or animals that live there.
ruined	total destruction or disintegration, either physical, moral, social, or economic	to damage beyond repair	to spoil or destroy something completely	To ruin something means to severely damage or spoil it.
dilapidated	having fallen into a state of disrepair or deterioration, as through neglect; broken-down and shabby	partly ruined or decayed especially from age or lack of care	old, broken, and in very bad condition	A building that is dilapidated is old and in a generally bad condition.

(cont.) |

Word	Source of definition			
	The American Heritage Dictionary of the English Language (Pickett et al., 2000)	*Word Central: Merriam–Webster Student's Electronic Dictionary* (2007)	*Longman Advanced American Dictionary* (Delacroix et al., 2007)	*Collins COBUILD Dictionary: English Language* (Sinclair et al., 1987)
uncanny	peculiarly unsettling, as if of supernatural origin or nature; eerie	being beyond what is normal	very strange and difficult to explain	You describe something as uncanny when it is strange and hard to explain.
distinguished	to cause oneself to be eminent or recognized	widely known and admired for excellence	very successful and therefore respected and admired	If you describe someone as distinguished or describe their work or career as distinguished, you mean that they have been very successful in their work or career and therefore have a high reputation.
astonishment	great surprise or amazement	to strike with sudden wonder or surprise	complete surprise	Astonishment is a feeling of great surprise.
malicious	having the nature of or resulting from malice; deliberately harmful; spiteful	doing mean things for pleasure	showing a desire to harm or hurt someone	Malicious talk or behavior is intended to harm a person or their reputation.
susceptible	easily influenced or affected	easily affected or impressed	easily influenced or affected by something	If you are susceptible to something you are likely to be influenced by it.

Word	Source of definition			
	The American Heritage Dictionary of the English Language (Pickett et al., 2000)	*Word Central: Merriam– Webster Student's Electronic Dictionary* (2007)	*Longman Advanced American Dictionary* (Delacroix et al., 2007)	*Collins COBUILD Dictionary: English Language* (Sinclair et al., 1987)
skeptical	marked by or given to doubt; questioning	relating to or marked by doubt	having doubts about whether something is true, right, or good	Someone who is skeptical about some-thing has a lot of doubts about it, for example, about how useful, true, or likely it is.

In the table below, we explain some of the adjustments we made to some of the *COBUILD* definitions.

COBUILD definition	Our definition	Our explanation
The *inhabitants* of a place are the people or animals that live there.	The inhabitants of a place are all the people who live there.	We mostly adopted the *COBUILD* features, but chose to limit it to people.
To *ruin* something means to severely damage or spoil it.	If something is ruined, it has been destroyed and it can't function or be used any longer.	We decided a bit more elaboration would be helpful in order to focus on the idea that something ruined no longer works.
A building that is *dilapidated* is old and in a generally bad condition.	Something dilapidated is falling apart and almost completely broken down.	We adopted and extended some of the *American Heritage* wording to create a more specified explanation—"falling apart" etc., especially to distinguish it from *ruined*.
You describe something as *uncanny* when it is strange and hard to explain.	If someone or something is uncanny, it is surprising and strange in almost a scary way.	We combined elements from *COBUILD* and *American Heritage* to include the ideas of both strange and eerie. *(cont.)*

COBUILD definition	Our definition	Our explanation
If you describe someone as *distinguished* or describe their work or career as distinguished, you mean that they have been very successful in their work or career and therefore have a high reputation.	People who are distinguished are highly respected and admired, usually for work they have done.	We thought about elements from all the definitions to come up with an explanation to include two ideas: that distinguished people are admired, and that it is for some accomplishment.
Astonishment is a feeling of great surprise.	If you express astonishment you feel suddenly shocked and surprised.	We added shock to the surprise element.

Creating Contexts for Using the Words That Go Beyond the Text

Engage

Contextualize each word in a different way—that is, provide a sentence that shows how each word can be used in a context or situation that is not the same as the one in the story.

Compare

Compare your new contexts with ours.

- We are all *inhabitants* of some town or city.
- You might *ruin* a white shirt by washing it with something red.
- Steps that are *dilapidated* would be dangerous to climb.
- It might seem *uncanny* if, whenever the fans cheered, the team scored.
- We would feel very lucky if a *distinguished* author came to talk to our class.
- You would probably be *astonished* if your teacher said there would be no more homework for the rest of the year.
- Trying to make people believe nasty and untrue things about someone would be *malicious*.
- People can be *susceptible* to believing things that they hope are true. *Susceptible* is also used to mean that you can get some sickness easily—like some people are susceptible to the flu.
- You might be *skeptical* if a friend who never took music lessons told you he was playing in a piano concert.

Consider and Reflect

The importance of an additional context should not be underestimated because it is often the case that people limit the use of a new word to the context in which they first encountered it. Thus, we always provide at least one additional context for each word in the Introduction portion of robust instruction. Do your additional contexts provide features of the word not included in the original story context? Do the contexts display other facets of how the words might be used?

Developing an Activity for Students to Interact with Word Meanings

The final step of the Introduction is to provide an opportunity for students to *interact* with the word. To this point the teacher has presented information to the students: contextualized the word, provided a friendly explanation, and provided an additional context. Thus, the students have only listened. So, in the introductory phase for each word, the last step is an activity in which students do something to actively engage with the word's meanings. If students don't *do* something, it is questionable whether much learning can occur.

Engage

Develop a short activity that requires students to interact with each word's meaning. Since this should be a quick activity, it is best not to require any writing. You might want to consult the Menu of Instructional Activities in Appendix A as well as some examples in Chapter 6.

Compare

Say "Inhabitant" if I describe a place that you would want to inhabit. If you wouldn't want to live there, say "No, thanks!" Students should be asked why they responded as they did.

- the North Pole
- a tropical island
- a city where all the food is free
- the world's most crowded city
- a town where everyone is a TV star

Consider and Reflect

We think that a quick example/nonexample of situations that fit or do not fit the target words works well in this step of the Introduction. You need to keep a couple things in mind to make this format most effective: base the content of the examples on experiences, places, and characters that students are familiar with, and always ask "Why?" so that thinking about the word and its uses is made public.

Putting the Introduction to *inhabitants* Together

Having discussed and asked you to engage in each of the steps in our Introduction phase one at a time, let's pause here and put all the parts together for introducing the word *inhabitants* as a way of illustrating how it would be presented in a lesson.

inhabitants

- *Contextualize*—The story is about the *inhabitants* of a little town.
- *Friendly Explanation*—The *inhabitants* of a place are all the people who live there.
- *Additional Context*—We are all *inhabitants* of some town or city.
- *Students engage with the word's meaning*—Say "Inhabitant" if I describe a place that you would want to be an inhabitant of. If you wouldn't want to live there, say "No, thanks!" Students should be asked why they responded as they did.
  - the North Pole
  - a tropical island
  - a city where all the food is free
  - the world's most crowded city
  - a town where everyone is a TV star

Follow-Up Interactions with the Words

After the words have been introduced, students need to interact with the words and their meanings on subsequent days. Recall that the goal of working with newly introduced words over several days is to keep new words in action for a while and, relatedly, to provide for frequent encounters. Additionally, continuing with newly introduced words for several days allows for enlarging the contexts in which students use the words, and for supporting more complex thinking and writing with the words.

In Appendix A, our Menu of Instructional Activities provides examples of the kinds of activities that we would develop after the Introduction. Each activity should take about 3 to 15 minutes per day for a six-word set, 5 to 20 minutes for an 8–10 word set, and 10 to 25 minutes for a 10–15 word set. Of course, these estimated times are affected by how much writing and small-group activities that are included.

Developing Three Days of Follow-Up Activities

Engage

For each of the words in *The Bridge on the River Clarinette*, develop two activities for each of 3 days that will get students to interact with each word's meaning.

It can help to start off the development of activities with some brainstorming of the kinds of topics you might associate with the words or how you might have students talk about and relate to the words. Below, we present some quick brainstorming about contexts and topics that might help in developing activities for the words from the *Bridge* story. As you can see, what we provide is not complete and systematic, but it's a start for your thinking. It's been our experience that such brainstorming starts to ignite thinking about the words. For example, when we are working together and one of us comes up with a good example, it seems to spur on the process and all of us begin to suggest ideas. So we offer the quick brainstorming below in that spirit.

- *Susceptible* and *skeptical* seem like words that could describe people's reactions to advertising. So an activity might be to read some advertisements (real and made-up ones) and ask students whether they would be *susceptible* or *skeptical* and why.
- We think that the concept of *dilapidated* might be familiar to students, but they use other expressions for it. So for activities around *dilapidated,* we might start by talking about ways to capture the meaning of *dilapidated,* such as "on its last legs," "run-down," or "wrecked." Then we could ask students to think of other things they would describe this way and what they would call them.
- It seems that *malicious* is a rich word for describing characters and the *Harry Potter* books are a good source for finding such characters. *Uncanny* can be added to the mix here. Teachers could ask students to use both words to describe a character or to tell how the two words apply to different characters.
- The word *inhabitants* offers an opportunity to explore morphology: *habitat, inhabit,* and *habit.*
- There are lots of ways things can be *ruined,* so we could take advantage of these as we develop activities (e.g., financial ruin, physical ruin, ruining someone's reputation, ancient ruins).

The brainstorming above in conjunction with your ideas and the Menu of Instructional Activities in Appendix A should serve as the grist for creating follow-up activities.

Compare

Look over the activity formats in the Menu that you used to develop your activities.

Consider and Reflect

As you look over your activities, consider:

- Are they sequenced from simpler to more complex—for example, beginning with ones that require briefer responses to contexts, and moving to students creating their own contexts and possibly to writing?
- Do you provide various ways for students to work and respond—for example, orally, with gestures, working with the whole class, or working in groups/ pairs?
- Are the words used in a variety of contexts so students get a full, well-rounded perspective on each word's use?
- Do the contexts used in the activities draw on students' interests and experiences?
- Are the activities interesting and fun?

Developing an Assessment

Engage

Develop an assessment for each of the words *inhabitants, ruined, dilapidated, uncanny, distinguished, astonishment, malicious, susceptible,* and *skeptical.* You can use the discussion of assessment in Chapter 3 as a resource.

Compare

Compare your assessment items with examples provided in Chapter 6.

Consider and Reflect

- Do the assessment items that you developed allow students to demonstrate their understanding of the words?
- Do the items reflect what you want to know about students' understanding of the words?
- Have you provided items that focus on contexts in which the words can be used appropriately, as well as on items that focus on the meanings of the words?

WORKING WITH A TEXT APPROPRIATE FOR STUDENTS IN GRADES 9–12

For developing vocabulary instruction for high school students, we present *The Oval Portrait* by Edgar Allan Poe. Poe was fascinated by language, often copying particularly interesting passages from writers whom he admired like Shakespeare and Milton. He is famous for his short stories, but he is also renowned for his poetry. Poe's poetic interests are revealed in the deliberate word choices he made as he wrote. Get ready for a sumptuous word palette as you read *The Oval Portrait*.

Selecting Tier Two Words

Engage

Read the story and mark any Tier Two words that you think are candidates for after-reading robust instruction. There's a reminder: there are lots of intriguing words in the story, so remember to select those that you think will have the most mileage for your students. We have identified 10 candidates.

The Oval Portrait
by Edgar Allan Poe

The chateau into which my valet had ventured to make forcible entrance, rather than permit me, in my desperately wounded condition, to pass a night in the open air, was one of those piles of commingled gloom and grandeur which have so long frowned among the Apennines, not less in fact than in the fancy of Mrs. Radcliffe. To all appearance it had been temporarily and very lately abandoned. We established ourselves in one of the smallest and least sumptuously furnished apartments. It lay in a remote turret of the building. Its decorations were rich, yet tattered and antique. Its walls were hung with tapestry and bedecked with manifold and multiform armorial trophies, together with an unusually great number of very spirited modern paintings in frames of rich golden arabesque. In these paintings, which depended from the walls not only in their main surfaces, but in very many nooks which the bizarre architecture of the chateau rendered necessary—in these paintings my incipient delirium, perhaps, had caused me to take deep interest; so that I bade Pedro to close the heavy shutters of the room—since it was already night—to light the tongues of a tall candelabrum which stood by the head of my bed—and to throw open far and wide the fringed curtains of black velvet which enveloped the bed itself. I wished all this done that I might resign myself, if not to sleep, at least alternately to the contemplation of these pictures, and the perusal of a small volume which had been found upon the pillow, and which purported to criticize and describe them.

Long—long I read—and devoutly, devotedly I gazed. Rapidly and gloriously the hours flew by, and the deep midnight came. The position of the candelabrum displeased me, and outreaching my hand with difficulty, rather than disturb my slumbering valet, I placed it so as to throw its rays more fully upon the book.

But the action produced an effect altogether unanticipated. The rays of the numerous candles (for there were many) now fell within a niche of the room which had hitherto been thrown into deep shade by one of the bed-posts. I thus saw in vivid light a picture all unnoticed before. It was the portrait of a young girl just ripening into womanhood. I glanced at the painting hurriedly, and then closed my eyes. Why I did this was not at first apparent even to my own perception. But while my lids remained thus shut, I ran over in mind my reason for so shutting them. It was an impulsive movement to gain time for thought—to make sure that my vision had not deceived me—to calm and subdue my fancy for a more sober and more certain gaze. In a very few moments I again looked fixedly at the painting.

That I now saw aright I could not and would not doubt; for the first flashing of the candles upon that canvas had seemed to dissipate the dreamy stupor which was stealing over my senses, and to startle me at once into waking life.

The portrait, I have already said, was that of a young girl. It was a mere head and shoulders, done in what is technically termed a *vignette* manner; much in the style of the favorite heads of Sully. The arms, the bosom and even the ends of the radiant hair, melted imperceptibly into the vague yet deep shadow which formed the background of the whole. The frame was oval, richly gilded and filigreed in *Moresque.* As a thing of art nothing could be more admirable than the painting itself. But it could have been neither the execution of the work, nor the immortal beauty of the countenance, which had so suddenly and so vehemently moved me. Least of all, could it have been that my fancy, shaken from its half slumber, had mistaken the head for that of a living person. I saw at once that the peculiarities of the design, of the *vignetting,* and of the frame, must have instantly dispelled such idea—must have prevented even its momentary entertainment. Thinking earnestly upon these points, I remained, for an hour perhaps, half sitting, half reclining, with my vision riveted upon the portrait. At length, satisfied with the true secret of its effect, I fell back within the bed. I had found the spell of the picture in an absolute life-likeliness of expression, which at first startling, finally confounded, subdued and appalled me. With deep and reverent awe I replaced the candelabrum in its former position. The cause of my deep agitation being thus shut from view, I sought eagerly the volume which discussed the paintings and their histories. Turning to the number which designated the oval portrait, I there read the vague and quaint words which follow:

"She was a maiden of rarest beauty, and not more lovely than full of glee. And evil was the hour when she saw, and loved, and wedded the painter. He, passionate, studious, austere, and having already a bride in his Art; she a maiden of rarest beauty, and not more lovely than full of glee: all light and smiles, and frolicsome as the young fawn: loving and cherishing all things: hating only the Art which was her rival: dreading only the pallet and brushes and other untoward instruments which deprived her of the countenance of her lover. It was thus a terrible thing for this lady to hear the painter speak of his desire to portray even his young bride. But she was humble and obedient, and sat meekly for many weeks in the dark high turret-chamber where the light dripped upon the pale canvas only from overhead. But he, the painter, took glory in his work, which went on from hour to hour and from day to day. And he was a passionate, and wild and moody man, who became lost in reveries; so that he *would* not see that the light which fell so ghastily in that lone turret withered the health and the spirits of his bride, who pined visibly to all but him. Yet she smiled on and still on, uncomplainingly, because she saw that the painter, (who had high renown,) took a fervid and burning pleasure in his task, and wrought day and night to depict her who so loved him, yet who grew daily more dispirited and weak. And in sooth some who beheld the portrait spoke of its resemblance in low words, as of a mighty marvel, and a proof not less of the power of the painter than of his deep love for her whom he depicted so surpassingly well. But at length, as the labor drew nearer to its conclusion, there were admitted none into the turret; for the painter had grown wild with the ardor of his work, and turned his eyes from the canvas rarely, even to regard the countenance of his wife. And he *would* not see that the tints which he spread upon the canvas were drawn from the cheeks of her who sate beside him. And when many weeks had passed, and but little remained to do, save one brush upon the mouth and one tint upon the eye, the spirit of the lady again flickered up as the flame within the socket of the lamp. And then the brush was given, and then the tint was placed; and, for one moment, the painter stood entranced before the work which he had wrought; but in the next, while he yet gazed he grew tremulous and very pallid, and aghast and crying with a loud voice, 'This is indeed *Life* itself!' turned suddenly to regard his beloved:—*She was dead!*"

Compare

What words did you select? We identified *sumptuously, bizarre, incipient, contemplation, purported, imperceptibly, vehemently, dispelled, riveted,* and *austere.*

Consider and Reflect

You've seen how incredible Poe's vocabulary is! The first sentence alone has at least eight words that could be considered Tier Two: *ventured, forcible, permit, desperately, commingled, gloom, grandeur,* and *fancy*—not to mention unfamiliar words such as *chateau* and *valet!* But let's stay focused on a set of useful and interesting words that are likely to be unfamiliar to high school students reading this text.

Perhaps you considered *confounded, tremulous,* and *pallid.* All are interesting words but we did not select them because they are closely related to words that students already know: *confounded* and *confused, tremulous* and *trembling, pallid* and *pale.*

You might think that students are already familiar with the word *bizarre.* We agree that high school students have probably heard this word and perhaps used it too. But the definition of the word offers an interesting example of how words are related to but differ from other words. *Bizarre* does not refer to something that is just unusual. Rather, *bizarre* includes the idea that something is extremely unconventional or hard to believe, something that can be described as "way out there." Providing opportunities for students to investigate similarities and differences among words is an excellent way for them to discover the precise way in which writers choose specific words for particular purposes.

Our choice of the word *dispel* may seem like an odd one. However, like *bizarre,* a thoughtful consideration of *dispel* reveals interesting shades of meaning. It most often is used to refer to driving away particular ideas or states of mind rather than to scattering people or objects. We considered using *dissipated,* which is very close in meaning to *dispel,* but decided against it because *dissipated* also has another meaning which is not related to the way the word is used in the story.

As we've mentioned before, selecting Tier Two words is largely a subjective enterprise—particularly when a text offers so many to choose from! There are several other Tier Two words that we might have chosen from *The Oval Portrait,* including *remote, resign* (oneself), *perusal, vivid, impulsive, subdue, appalled,* and *agitation.* We decided not to select *remote* because students probably have the idea and can connect it to the remote control of their TVs. Likewise, we thought that students probably have a more than passing acquaintance with the words *impulsive, subdue, appalled,* and *agitation.* However, we could very well have chosen *resign, perusal,* and *vivid.* Those words have mileage and could enhance student writing as well. Choice plays a part in making decisions, and our choice was to focus on the words that we listed above.

Selecting Words about the Story

We have discussed that selections of words to teach might come not from the story itself, but be *about* the story. In this case, selecting words about the story might be . . . bizarre, because Poe provides so many outstanding choices within the story! But if you want some discussion on that topic, in case it is useful for other texts you might work with, you can refer to the other stories in this chapter. There are discussions of words about the story in each of them.

Let's assume that we will work with the words *sumptuously, bizarre, incipient, contemplation, purported, imperceptibly, vehemently, dispelled, riveted,* and *austere.*

Introducing the Words

Robust vocabulary instruction can be divided into two stages: Introduction and Follow-up. The Introduction occurs after the selection has been read. The Follow-up occurs on subsequent days. First, we will deal with each of the components in our Introductions, which include the features noted in earlier sections and repeated below. We will ask you to engage in each introductory component.

- contextualizing the word
- providing a student-friendly explanation
- presenting alternative contexts for the word
- inviting students to interact with the word in a meaningful way

Contextualizing the Words Based on Their Use in the Text

Engage

Contextualize each word—that is, provide a sentence that describes how each word is used in the story.

Compare

Compare your sentences with ours.

- In the story, the narrator and his valet made their way to a room in the chateau that was one of the smallest and least *sumptuously* decorated.
- The narrator described the architecture of the chateau as *bizarre.*
- The narrator felt that his *incipient* delirium was causing him to become overly interested in the paintings in the room.
- Because he was confined to a bed, the narrator had time to *contemplate* the paintings in the room.
- In the story, the narrator found a book that *purported* to describe the paintings.
- As he looked at the oval portrait, the narrator noted that the head and shoulders of the young woman blended *imperceptibly* into the dark background of the painting.
- The narrator began to question the *vehement* feelings that the portrait evoked in him.
- He realized that the way the picture was painted as well as its frame instantly *dispelled* from his mind the idea that there was a living person in the room.
- His attention was *riveted* by the portrait and he continued looking at it for almost an hour.
- The book about the paintings included a description of the artist who was said to be an *austere* man.

Consider and Reflect

Since the words come from or are about a particular story, contextualizing the words is a pretty straightforward step. The only point that may vary is the extent to which you use the exact wording of the story. You may want to alter the wording to make it more conversational or to focus more squarely on the target word. As can be seen above, we have done it several ways. We think it's a good idea to change the wording within a set of target words so the context isn't presented in a formulaic way.

Crafting Student-Friendly Explanations

Engage

Develop a student-friendly explanation for each word.

Compare

Compare your explanations with ours.

- Something that is *sumptuous* is magnificent and obviously expensive.
- Something that is *bizarre* is so out of the ordinary or unconventional that is it weird and a little scary.
- If something is *incipient* that means that it is just beginning to appear or exist or happen.
- To *contemplate* something or someone means to look at them for a long time, thoughtfully and steadily observing them and thinking about or considering them.
- If someone or something *purports* to do or be a particular thing, they claim to do or be that thing, or they have the reputation of doing or being that thing.
- Something that is *imperceptible* is almost impossible to see or notice because it is so slight, or gradual, or subtle.
- *Vehement* feelings and opinions are strongly held and forcefully expressed.
- If you *dispel* an idea or feeling, you stop people from believing in it or feeling it.
- If you are *riveted* by something, it fascinates you and holds your interest completely.
- An *austere* person is strict and serious, stern and cold.

Consider and Reflect

As we have discussed in *Bringing Words to Life* and elsewhere in this volume (see Chapter 3, p. 23), we have adopted a specific style for presenting word meanings that we call "student-friendly explanations." The easiest way to develop friendly explanations is to use the *COBUILD Dictionary*, making any adjustments as needed for the language level of the students or the sense that you want to focus on. If you do not have a *COBUILD Dictionary* available, friendly explanations can be developed by working with traditional dictionary definitions and transforming the language. To aid the thinking process involved in developing friendly explanations, below we present the definitions from four dictionaries for the 10 words from *The Oval Portrait*.

You will notice that some of the words did not appear in *COBUILD*. Here we encounter one of this dictionary's limitations: it has a smaller corpus than traditional dictionaries, and thus does not include some of the words we want to teach at upper-grade levels.

Word	Source of definition			
	The American Heritage Dictionary of the English Language (Pickett et al., 2000)	*Word Central: Merriam–Webster Student's Electronic Dictionary* (2007)	*Longman Advanced American Dictionary* (Delacroix et al., 2007)	*Collins COBUILD Dictionary: English Language* (Sinclair et al., 1987)
sumptuous	of a size or splendor suggesting great expense; lavish	extremely costly, rich, luxurious, or magnificent	very impressive and expensive	Something that is sumptuous is magnificent and obviously expensive.
bizarre	strikingly unconventional and far-fetched in style or appearance; odd	strikingly out of the ordinary as a: odd, extravagant, or eccentric in style or mode; b: involving sensational contrasts or incongruities	very unusual or strange	Something that is bizarre is very odd and strange.
incipient	beginning to exist or appear	beginning to come into being or to become apparent	starting to happen or exist	(Not included)
contemplation	thoughtful observation or study	the act of considering with attention; the act of regarding steadily	quiet serious thinking about something	To contemplate something or someone means to look at them for a long time.
purported	assumed to be such; supposed	reputed; alleged	to claim to be or do something, even if this is not true	If someone or something purports to do or be a particular thing, they claim to do or be that thing. *(cont.)*

Word	Source of definition			
	The American Heritage Dictionary of the English Language (Pickett et al., 2000)	*Word Central: Merriam–Webster Student's Electronic Dictionary* (2007)	*Longman Advanced American Dictionary* (Delacroix et al., 2007)	*Collins COBUILD Dictionary: English Language* (Sinclair et al., 1987)
imperceptibly	impossible or difficult to perceive by the mind or senses; so subtle, slight, or gradual as to be barely perceptible	not perceptible by a sense or by the mind: extremely slight, gradual, or subtle	almost impossible to see or notice	(Not included)
vehemently	characterized by forcefulness of expression or intensity of emotion or conviction; marked by or full of vigor or energy	marked by forceful energy as a: intensely emotional; b: deeply felt, forcibly expressed; c: bitterly antagonistic	showing very strong feelings or opinions	Vehement feelings and opinions are strongly held and forcefully expressed.
dispelled	to rid one's mind of; to drive away or off by or as if by scattering	to drive away by or as if by scattering	to make something go away, especially a belief, idea, or feeling	To dispel an idea or feeling means to stop people believing in it or feeling it.
riveted	to engross or hold the attention	to attract and hold	if your attention is riveted on something, you are so interested or so frightened that you cannot move	If you are riveted by something, it fascinates you and holds your interest completely.

Word	Source of definition			
	The American Heritage Dictionary of the English Language (Pickett et al., 2000)	*Word Central: Merriam–Webster Student's Electronic Dictionary* (2007)	*Longman Advanced American Dictionary* (Delacroix et al., 2007)	*Collins COBUILD Dictionary: English Language* (Sinclair et al., 1987)
austere	severe or stern in disposition or appearance; somber and grave	stern and cold in appearance or manner; somber, grave	Someone who is austere is very strict and serious—used to show disapproval. An austere way of life is very simple and has few things to make it comfortable or enjoyable.	An austere person is strict and serious. An austere way of life is rather harsh, with no luxuries.

In the table below, we explain some of the adjustments we made to some of the *COBUILD* definitions.

COBUILD definition	Our definition	Our explanation
Something that is *bizarre* is very odd and strange.	Something that is *bizarre* is out of the ordinary or unconventional.	We wanted to provide a more precise and sophisticated explanation for *bizarre* to emphasize its particular use in reference to things that are not the way they usually are.
There was no definition for *incipient* provided in the *COBUILD Dictionary*.	If something is *incipient* that means that it is just beginning to appear or exist or happen.	We made use of the definitions provided by the *American Heritage* and *Longman* dictionaries.
To *contemplate* something or someone means to look at them for a long time.	To *contemplate* something or someone means to look at them for a long time, thoughtfully and steadily observing them.	We adopted the *COBUILD* definition but added the idea of thoughtful and steady observation from the *American Heritage* and *Merriam–Webster* dictionaries to emphasize that contemplating is more than just looking.
		(cont.)

COBUILD definition	Our definition	Our explanation
There was no definition for *imperceptible* provided in the *COBUILD Dictionary*.	Something that is *imperceptible* is almost impossible to see or notice because it is so slight, or gradual, or subtle.	We used elements from the *American Heritage, Merriam–Webster,* and *Longman* dictionaries to capture the idea that something *imperceptible* is almost impossible to see and the reason for that is because the something is slight, or gradual, or subtle.
An *austere* person is strict and serious.	An *austere* person is strict and serious, stern and cold.	We adopted the *COBUILD* definition but also included the notions of sternness and coldness from the *Merriam–Webster Dictionary* in order to make the definition more related to the kind of feelings an austere person would exude.

Creating Contexts for Using the Words That Go Beyond the Text

Engage

Contextualize each word in a different way—that is, provide a sentence that describes how each word is used in a context or situation that is not the same as the one in the story.

Compare

Compare your new contexts with ours.

- If you went to a five-star restaurant, you would expect a *sumptuous* meal.
- A hair style that had multicolored sections of different lengths might be described as *bizarre*.
- Many animals and even plants can sense an *incipient* storm and react in a variety of ways.
- You can *contemplate* a phrase in a poem, trying to interpret its meaning or just enjoying the words the poet chose and the way they sound.
- Someone might post the *purported* ending of a new novel before it was published, but it could turn out to be false.
- Music at a noisy party might seem *imperceptible*.

- During a debate, presidential candidates might speak more and more *vehemently* in defense of their positions.
- A teacher's explanation can help to *dispel* students' confusion and frustration.
- I've seen students *riveted* by the earliest editions of comic books, including ones about the Flash and Wonder Woman.
- A starkly furnished apartment might be evidence of an *austere* life.

Consider and Reflect

The importance of an additional context should not be underestimated because it is not that uncommon for people to limit the use of a new word to the context in which they first encountered it. Thus, we always provide at least one additional context for each word that we want students to learn. We also encourage students to come up with their own additional contexts as they interact with the words throughout each week's lessons. Do your additional contexts provide features of the word not included in the original story context? Does it provide another facet of how the word might be used?

Developing an Activity for Students to Interact with Word Meanings

The final step of the Introduction is to provide an opportunity for students to *interact* with the word. To this point, the teacher has presented information to the students: contextualized the word, provided a friendly explanation, and presented an additional context. Thus, the students have only listened. So in the introductory phase for each word, the last step is an activity in which students *do* something to actively engage with the words' meanings. If students don't *do* something, it is questionable whether much learning can occur.

Engage

Develop a short activity that requires students to interact with each word's meaning. Since this should be a quick activity, it is best not to require any writing. You might want to consult the Menu of Instructional Activities in Appendix A as well as some examples in Chapter 6.

Compare

Compare your idea for introducing the words with the example below. Select the objects or situations that might be described by the word *sumptuous,* and explain the reason for your choice.

- a used-car lot
- the entrance to a museum

- the binding of a very expensive and rare book
- community vegetable gardens
- the dressing room of an upscale boutique

Consider and Reflect

We thought a quick example/nonexample of a situation or item that could or could not be described as *sumptuous* worked well in this step of the Introduction. Keep in mind this advice to make this format most effective: base the examples on experiences that students are familiar with, and always remember to ask students to explain their responses.

Putting the Introduction to *sumptuous* Together

Having discussed and asked you to engage in each of the steps in our Introduction phase one at a time, let's pause here and put all the parts together for the word *sumptuous* as a way of illustrating how one would be presented in a lesson.

sumptuous

- *Contextualize*—In the story, the narrator and his valet made their way to a room in the chateau that was one of the smallest and least *sumptuously* decorated.
- *Friendly Explanation*—Something that is *sumptuous* is magnificent and obviously expensive.
- *Additional Context*—If you went to a five-star restaurant, you would expect a *sumptuous* meal.
- *Students engage with the word's meaning*—Select the objects or situations that might be described by the word *sumptuous,* and explain the reason for your choice.
  - a used-car lot
  - the entrance to a museum
  - the binding of a very expensive and rare book
  - community vegetable gardens
  - the dressing room of an upscale boutique

Follow-Up Interactions with the Words

After the words have been introduced, students need to interact with the words and their meanings on subsequent days. Recall that the goal of working with newly introduced words over several days is to keep new words in action for a while and, relatedly, to provide for frequent encounters. Additionally, continuing with newly introduced words for several days allows for enlarging the contexts in which students use the words, and for supporting more complex thinking and writing with the words.

Appendix A, the Menu of Instructional Activities, provides examples of the kinds of activities that we would develop after the Introduction has occurred. Each activity should take about 3 to 15 minutes per day for a six-word set, 5 to 20 minutes for an 8–10 word set, and 10 to 25 minutes for a 10–15 word set. Of course, these estimated times are affected by how much writing and how many small-group activities you choose to use.

Developing Three Days of Follow-Up Activities

Engage

For each of the words in *The Oval Portrait*, develop two activities for each of 3 days that will get students to interact with each word's meaning.

It can help to start off the development of activities with some brainstorming of the kinds of topics you might associate with the words or how you might have students talk about and relate to the words. Below we present some quick brainstorming about contexts and topics that might help you in developing activities for the words from *The Oval Portrait*. As you can see, what we provide is not complete and systematic, but it's a start for your thinking. It's been our experience that such starts ignite thinking about the words. For example, when we are working together and one of us comes up with a good example, it seems to spur on the process and all of us begin to suggest ideas. So we offer the quick brainstorming below in that spirit.

- *Austere* and *sumptuous* seem like good candidates for comparing and contrasting words that can describe surroundings, food, clothing, and lifestyle.
- Students can write about things that leave them *riveted* from categories such as music, literature, and video games. *Bizarre* would also be related here by students discussing how they might be *riveted* by things that are *bizarre*.
- Students can describe why the following can be viewed as *incipient*:
  - the spring
  - a first date
  - a seed
  - a gray hair
- Challenge students to fill in words on a continuum describing ways of thinking about something. The end points could be "a passing thought" and "contemplate." Where would they put, for example, *consider, ponder, wonder,* and *puzzle over.* They could also provide an example of something they would think about in each "way of thinking."

The brainstorming above in conjunction with your ideas and the Menu of Instructional Activities in Appendix A should serve as the grist for creating follow-up activities.

Compare

Compare your activities with those presented in the Menu of Instructional Activities.

Consider and Reflect

As you look over your activities, consider:

- Are they sequenced from simpler to more complex—that is, do you begin with activities that require briefer responses to contexts, and move to having students create their own contexts and possibly write?
- Do you provide various ways for students to work and respond? For example, do students have opportunities to speak and perform, or to work alone or with a partner?
- Are the words used in a variety of contexts so students get a full, well-rounded perspective on each word's use?
- Do the contexts used in the activities draw on students' interests and experiences?
- Are the activities interesting and fun?

Developing an Assessment

Engage

Develop an assessment for each of the words. Check the discussion of assessment in Chapter 3.

Compare

Compare your assessment items with examples provided in Chapter 6.

Consider and Reflect

- Do the assessment items that you developed allow students to demonstrate their understanding of the words?
- Do the items reflect what you want to know about students' understanding of the words?
- Have you provided items that focus on contexts in which the words can be used appropriately as well as items that focus on the meanings of the words?

APPENDIX A

* * * * * * *

Menu of Instructional Activities

This menu provides examples of instructional activities that you can use to engage students in interacting with the vocabulary words they are learning. We have included seven categories of activities, with from two to five variations within some categories. They are:

- Example/nonexample, with five variations
- Word associations, with three variations
- Generating Situations, Contexts, and Examples, with five variations
- Word relationships, with five variations
- Writing, with three variations
- Returning to the Story Context
- Puzzles, with two variations

In some cases, all the words in a set of vocabulary words can be used within one variation of an activity. In other cases, only some of those words are suited for a particular variation. When that happens, to provide opportunities to work with all the words in a set each day, you may need to include several variations within a category of activities, or you may need to include another category of activity.

In virtually all the activities that follow, each item (question or statement) is really "bait" for students to use language to explain their responses. Most students can answer questions like "Which would make you feel *drowsy*: watching your favorite TV program or eating a big Thanksgiving dinner?" It's what needs to come after—an explanation for their choices—that is the most useful for vocabulary, and indeed, language development. The forced-choice activities and questions are usually designed such that there is an expected response. For example, if we ask "When might you be reluctant—going into a dentist's office or going into a toy store?" we expect that students will say "dentist's office." But the most important part is the requirement to explain why: "Because having your teeth worked on is no fun, so you might not want to go in!" However, if a student chooses the less likely response and can justify it—

such as choosing toy store "Because I'm trying to save my money and I'm afraid I'd want to buy something"—then, by all means, accept that response. The important point to stress here is *if they can justify it.* It is not acceptable to choose toy store because, for example, "I like toy stores." The justification must relate to the target word.

For the most part, we see the activities as teacher-led—that is, we do not advocate regularly converting the activities into workbook pages. Occasionally that can be appropriate if the teacher goes over the work with the class. Also, sometimes activities can be used by assigning students to groups: the students in each group can do the same thing and then come together as a whole group and discuss the similarities and differences between different groups' responses. Or different activities can be assigned to separate groups and then shared with the whole group. Although some activities (e.g., analogies) may be somewhat beyond the capacities of the youngest students, most activities are appropriate for all levels, with the difference being in the words and contexts that are used.

We have arranged the categories of activities in this menu generally from simple to more complex. By that we mean that the categories of activities begin with those that provide the most guidance for student responses and expect the most simple responses from them. From there, the thinking and responding expected becomes more complex—as students are asked to develop contexts, consider relationships between words, respond in writing, and so on.

EXAMPLE/NONEXAMPLE

Asking students to indicate which statements, descriptions, comments, or the like are instances of a given vocabulary word and which ones are not is a prototypical early interactive activity. We use Example/Nonexample in some of our activities in Chapter 6 as well as in the activities for the four texts that we included as the basis for professional development.

Variation 1

Below is a version we use very often, which presents, one by one, descriptions of situations and asks students to respond to each as to whether or not it illustrates the target word. Students should always be asked "why?" they responded as they did.

- If I say something that sounds *precarious,* say "Precarious." If not, don't say anything. Students should be asked why they responded as they did.
  - Walking over a rickety bridge that spans a deep canyon
  - Exploring a new tall school building
  - Standing on a tall ladder on one foot

Notice that in this format students are asked to say the target word, which is helpful in getting them to build a strong phonological representation of the words they are learning. That's important for helping to plant the word in students' memories.

Variation 2

A simple variation on the basic Example/Nonexample presented above is to add a little creativity to how students indicate their response. Ask "why?"

- If any of the things I say are examples of places where it might be *frigid,* say "Brrrr." If not, don't say anything:
  - Antarctica
  - Florida
  - Canada in January
  - Mexico
- If any of the things I say are things that might be *sleek,* say "Smooth, man." If not, don't say anything:
  - a porcupine
  - a duck
  - a leaf
  - a car

Variation 3

Another variation on the Example/Nonexample activity that we use quite often asks students to choose which of two alternatives illustrates the target word. This variation is usually presented as *Which would . . . ?* or *Which is . . . ?* Ask "why?"

- Which would be easier to *notice*:
  - a house all alone on a hill or a house crowded in with lots of other buildings
  - a barking dog or a dog sleeping on a porch
  - an ant crawling along the floor or a snake slithering along the floor
- Which would *plod*:
  - Frankenstein in a castle or a ghost in a castle
  - a huge dinosaur or a mountain lion
  - a heavy man or a skinny man
  - a girl who was really tired or a girl in a race
- Which would make a house *festive*: colorful banners hanging outside or turning the lights off?
- Which could make you scream *frantically*: a kitten purring or a snake hissing?
- Which is more *absurd*: a dog wearing glasses or a dog snoring?
- Which is more *versatile*: a heavy fur coat or a coat with a zip-in lining? Why?

Variation 4

Another variation within the Example/Nonexample activity asks students to choose which of two target words represents a situation that is described. This is somewhat more challenging as it asks students to bring to mind meanings of two target words and decide which fits. Several examples follow.

- Would you want the people who cook the school lunch to be *versatile* or *frugal*? Why?
- If you didn't buy a pair of shoes until you wore out the ones you had, would that be *frugal* or *industrious*? Why?
- If you just won the lottery, would you be *jubilant* or *melancholy*? Why?

The format below is a minor variation of the ones above. However, the wording may be helpful when developing activities for some words.

- Which would be something to *resist*:
  - Talking to a stranger or helping a companion? Why?
  - Laughing at someone's joke or laughing at someone's mistake? Why?

Variation 5

Here is a final variation on Example/Nonexample activity that is useful for drawing attention to the distinguishing features of words that may get confused with each other:

- If you had a very special photograph of a friend who had moved away, would you refer to it as a *memento* or a *talisman*? Why?
- If you had a special keychain, a kind of lucky charm, would you refer to it as a *memento* or as a *talisman*? Why?

WORD ASSOCIATIONS

Word association is another type of activity that gives students something to respond to by relating what is presented with one of the target words. Such activities provide another opportunity for students to make connections between new words and people, happenings, and other things familiar to them. The kind of word association we use differs from the traditional method in which students associate a target word with a definition or synonym. Rather, we up the ante a bit by asking students to associate words with a conversational expression. This method is more challenging because it does not ask for such a direct association as a definition, but requires some interpretation.

Variation 1

With the words *tedious, extravagant,* and *pretentious,* you might ask which of the following comments goes with a target word.

- I spent all my allowance for 6 months on that video.
- I just can't face another minute of this!
- You're so lucky that I am part of your team.

Variation 2

Ask students to come up with an association—it can be a person, a movie, a common experience—to target words, and then explain the connection they see. This activity, as is the case for most of our examples, is meant to be done under teacher guidance. This is especially important in the earlier grades as the teacher can help students express their reasons for the association.

Word	Associations	Reasons/explanation
eloquent	*President Kennedy*	*Kennedy was an excellent speaker. People still talk about his speeches.*
pervasive	*Computer viruses*	*Viruses seem to be all over the place and you always have to be on the watch for them.*
fidelity	*Having the same best friend all your life*	*You are always faithful to that person.*

Variation 3

In this variation—idea substitution—students hear a sentence that has something to do with one of their words, and then indicate which word. They then revise the sentence in a way that includes the word.

- I didn't want to answer his questions so I pretended I didn't hear him. Which new word goes with that sentence? (*evade*) I didn't want to answer his questions so I *evaded* him.
- Milk is something that babies have to have. (*necessity*) Milk is a *necessity* for babies.
- My mother said I had really worked hard when I cleaned the whole house. Which new word goes with that sentence? (*industrious*) My mother said that I was *industrious* when I cleaned the whole house.

GENERATING SITUATIONS, CONTEXTS, AND EXAMPLES

In this next set of activities students are not provided with choices as in the example/ nonexample and the simple word association activities described above. Rather, students are asked to generate appropriate contexts or situations for statements or questions about their words. Generating language may prompt more elaborated thinking.

Variation 1

The following questions constrain the request for a situation within a specific context: the classroom. In other words, it holds the situation constant and challenges students to find ways to apply different target words to it.

- What would make a teacher say this to her class?:
  - What an *industrious* class you are!
  - What a *clever* class you are!
  - What a *splendid* class you are!
  - What a *versatile* class you are!

Variation 2

The questions below require developing situations across various contexts.

- What might a *clever* dog learn to do when his owner comes home?
- What would a *splendid* day for ducks look like?
- Why is eating leftovers a *frugal* thing to do?
- Why might you *examine* an apple you found on the street?

Variation 3

In the following format, we ask students to develop comments that people might make that are associated with target words.

- What might an audience say about a *splendid* musician?
- What might a generous person say to a *miser*?
- What might someone who is *exuberant* say about your new bike?
- What might someone who is *frugal* say when looking at the price tag on a coat?

Variation 4

Variations within this format are good for small-group collaborative work. For example, you might divide the class into four groups and have each group respond to the different portions of the following:

How might a . . . cook . . . a musician . . . a basketball player . . . a teacher show they are:

- *versatile*
- *industrious*
- *clever*
- *expert*

Variation 5

Another small-group activity might ask for different groups to develop descriptions of:

- three things that would be *catastrophic*
- three things that would be *preposterous*
- three ways that a gymnast is *flexible*
- three things a *philanthropist* might do

Of course, an important part of these activities is discussing the different groups' responses together. You might encourage more creative responses by telling students that they will get points for ideas that are different from another group's.

WORD RELATIONSHIPS

Having students think about and respond to how two words might be related is a strong activity for developing rich word knowledge. Working with two words and how their meanings and features might interact prompts students to explore novel contexts for the words and build new connections. These activities are pretty wide-open—you simply need to give the students a pair of words and see what happens! Some possibilities follow.

Variation 1

Ask students to describe how two vocabulary words might be connected or related. For example:

- *conscientious/haphazard*—A response might be something like: "Someone who is *conscientious* would not do things in a *haphazard* way."
- *compassionate/advocate*—A *compassionate* lawyer might act as an *advocate* for someone who is in need and otherwise could not afford a lawyer.

Variation 2

The activity above can be given more structure by phrasing a question around two words and asking students to respond and then explain their answers. For example:

- Do people with *prestige prosper*?
- What might a *meticulous* person be *vulnerable* to?
- Could someone who is *curious* be a *nuisance*?

Variation 3

Analogies are another form of word relationship. You can develop some, leaving one part for students to fill in. Eventually students can be asked to construct their own—either complete or with a part missing for other students to complete. Here are some examples.

- A *determined* person is someone who is really set on getting something done, while a person who is *wavering* is . . .
- You could describe someone as *morose* if he always saw the bad side of things. On the other hand, you could describe someone as *jovial* if she . . .

Variation 4

Another way to prompt students to think about relationships between words is to ask them to sort words. Here's where a Vocabulary Log (see Chapter 4) will come in handy. After students have been introduced to a number of words, encourage them to sort the words into various categories—any categories you can think of will do. The resulting lists could then be used as references when students are writing.

For example, students might group words as follows:

Words that describe people	Words that describe places
determined	tranquil
charming	eerie
impatient	monotonous
meek	rustic
eminent	exotic

Variation 5

Continuums and other formats for expressing amount or degree are other forms of word relationships. One of our favorites is the word line—because it can be used with any handful of words, and the end points of the continuum can be anything at all!

Ask students to place phrases (by number) on a word line that represents a continuum and to explain their placement. For example:

How surprised would you be if:

- An extremely *fragile* plant survived in an arctic region?
- An *enthusiastic* teacher came to school dressed in a pirate costume?
- A *determined* student gets an excellent grade?

Least surprised ——————————————————————— Most surprised

The word line format allows you to be as creative as you like! Here is a silly one:

I can handle it ——————————————————————— Can't handle it!

1. Having to *evade* someone you dislike every day
2. Everyone in the class thinks your outfit is *appalling*
3. Being *vulnerable* to a stomach flu
4. Your best friend is suddenly *reluctant* to talk to you

Here are just a few word line extremes we have seen teachers use:

pleasing ——————————————————————— disgusting
easy ——————————————————————— hard
calm ——————————————————————— scary
lame ——————————————————————— cool

Variation 5

There are other simple formats for having students respond about extent or degree of something about their words. For example:

- Clap to show how much (not at all, a little bit, a lot) you would like:
  - to have your project described by the word *preposterous*
  - working in a *chaotic* atmosphere to complete your big test
  - having your room described as *eerie*

WRITING

As students move beyond the early primary grades, a goal of a vocabulary program will surely include having them use their words in writing. The following examples are formats that can be used to encourage thoughtful responses and uses of the words as students write.

Variation 1

Provide students with sentence stems, such as the ones below, and ask them to complete them. The value of this format is that students can't just write the obvious ("The King was miserable") from which no one can tell whether a student understands the word. The *because* requires students to explain "why?"

- The King was *miserable* because . . .
- The Queen was *calm* because . . .
- The child was *perplexed* because . . .

There are many ways that this activity can be implemented in the classroom. For starters, students could complete the sentences individually or in collaborative pairs or groups. Another possibility is assigning several words to groups of students and have them create stems. They then switch papers with another group and complete the stems of their peers.

Variation 2

More extended writing can be generated by formats such as:

- Think of a time when you felt either *diligent, envious,* or *placid.* Write a little bit about what made you feel that way.
- Think of when you might need to *investigate, cooperate,* or be *impressive.* Write a paragraph to tell about it.
- Think of someone you could describe as one of the following: *precocious, meticulous, tenacious.* Tell what that person is like.

Variation 3

You can prompt students to use several of their words in a writing assignment by providing an interesting premise and asking them to use three, four, or five of their vocabulary words in the story. Some of our favorites:

- Going to the mall and all the lights go out
- Arriving in a new city and people think you are a celebrity
- Finding a puppy with a bag of money tied around its neck at your door

RETURNING TO THE STORY CONTEXT

Having students return to the original context in which they met the vocabulary words, the story, is a powerful way to reinforce the connection between understanding vocabulary and understanding story ideas. For example, below are two questions about *The Watsons Go to Birmingham—1963* (Curtis, 1995).

1. When Kenny came to read in Mr. Alums's room, Mr. Alums said to Byron: "If, instead of trying to *intimidate* your young brother, you would *emulate* him and try to use that mind of yours, perhaps you'd find things much easier" (p. 24). What did he mean?
   - Find examples of *intimidation* throughout the novel.
   - Find examples of people that Kenny and Byron try to *emulate*.
2. In his epilogue, Christopher Paul Curtis wrote: "In the Northern, Eastern, and Western states, African Americans often faced *discrimination,* but it was not as extreme and *pervasive* as in the South" (p. 207). What did he mean?
   - Find examples of *discrimination* mentioned in the novel.

We provided an example of another way to return to the story for young students in Chapter 6.

PUZZLES

Students always seem to enjoy puzzles that lead them through clues to an answer.

- Provide a series of clues for a vocabulary word. Each clue should narrow the range of possible responses. For example, the following sets of clues lead to the words *spectator, reliable,* and *relinquish*

   1. A lot of people would not actually see this person.
   2. It's someone who just watches.
   3. The word has nine letters and starts with an *s*_____.

   1. Baby-sitters need to be _____.
   2. If someone is _____ you can count on them.
   3. The word has eight letters and starts with an *r*_____.

1. It is hard for dogs to do this with a delicious bone.
2. This word means to "give something up."
3. This word has nine letters and starts with an *r*_____.

When students have some experience with this format, they can create the series of clues.

- Teachers seem to be partial to crossword puzzles, but comment that they take a great deal of time to develop. The website below provides a crossword puzzle generator. Older students can generate them too. In fact, that may be more valuable than completing a puzzle. Provide students with a list of words and after they develop a puzzle, have them exchange it with a partner, so that each student completes a puzzle. *www.edhelper.com/crossword.htm*

And don't forget drawing and dramatizing (see Chapter 4). These are not necessarily characteristic of robust instruction, but they can be used in robust ways. That is, always ask children to explain and discuss their responses.

APPENDIX B

****

Some Well-Known Books and Stories and Corresponding Tier Two Word Candidates

We selected Tier Two vocabulary words from the books and stories listed below to serve as examples of the opportunities for vocabulary development that these texts provide. The books in the Kindergarten–Grade 2 list are for reading aloud. The books in the other lists are ones that students could read themselves. We listed the words in the order in which they appear in each selection.

KINDERGARTEN–GRADE 2		
Book/author/publisher	**Vocabulary words**	
Amelia and Eleanor Go for a Ride by Pam Muñoz Ryan Scholastic	outspoken daring practical solo	determined elegant marveled hesitated
The Bee Tree by Patricia Polacco Putnam	charming commotion expedition sprinted	raucous savored wisdom pursue
Click, Clack, Moo: Cows That Type by Doreen Cronin Scholastic	strike impatient furious demand	neutral ultimatum exchange

Book/author/publisher	Vocabulary words	
Dinosaur Bob and His Adventures with the Family Lazardo by William Joyce HarperCollins	routine envy menace meekly	disturbing eventful hero startled
The Dinosaurs of Waterhouse Hawkins by Barbara Kerley HarperCollins	thwarted passion monumental erected	eminent anticipation solemn lavish
Her Seven Brothers by Paul Goble Bradbury	intend distant marveled faithful	immensity peering insists rage
If the Shoe Fits by Gary Soto Putnam	fabric pout refused glinted	demanded suave remarked protested
In Coal Country by Judith Hendershot Knopf	grime disagreeable huddled smoldered	straining familiar vibration repair
Johnny Appleseed: A Tall Tale by Steven Kellogg Morrow	surrounding boisterous tranquil replenish	affectionately urged recollections exaggerated
Lon Po Po: A Red-Riding Hood Story from China by Ed Young Putnam	dusk disguised route cunning	plump clever tender paced
No Star Nights by Anna Egan Smucker Knopf	operated billowing crouch glinted	spanned straining exhausted
The Pot That Juan Built by Nancy Andres-Goebel Lee & Low Books	vanished impoverished prosperous inspired	abundant available ancient cherishes
Roberto Clemente: Pride of the Pittsburgh Pirates by Jonah Winter Atheneum	denied professional style mocked	respect sneering hero victims

Book/author/publisher	Vocabulary words	
Stellaluna by Janell Cannon Harcourt	sultry scent clutched clambered	gracefully anxious peculiar gasped
The Stonecutter by Pam Newton Putnam	soared splendor luxury discontent	gratitude transformed boasted contentment
Two Bad Ants by Chris Van Allsburg Houghton Mifflin	swiftly remarkable eager delicate	vanished unaware calm stunned
The Ugly Duckling by Jerry Pinkney Houghton Mifflin	harmony secluded taunted comforting	floundered bewilderment companion miserable
When Marian Sang by Pam Muñoz Ryan Scholastic	prejudice unwavering humiliations endured	dignity awe restrictions trepidation
Yeh-Shen: A Cinderella Story from China by Ai-Ling Louie Philomel	dim crafty grief transformation	resemble entranced undaunted timidly
Zen Shorts by Jon J. Muth Scholastic	nuisance slight rummaging startled lamented	sympathy misfortune brooding preoccupied

GRADES 3–5

Book/author/publisher	Vocabulary words		
Frindle by Andrew Clemens Aladdin	reputation maximum concentration	alert disruption standards	controversial endures
The Higher Power of Lucky by Susan Patron Atheneum	*Chapters 1–3* anonymous suspense drastic sinister envisioned traits	*Chapters 4–6* remedy abandoned impression contribute interpretations surplus	*Chapters 7–9* dramatic gruesome unique repulsive dedicated alert

Book/author/publisher	Vocabulary words		
The Higher Power of Lucky (cont.)	*Chapters 10–12* memorial intricate jolting panic delicacy elegance teeming	*Chapters 13–15* frustrated dignified certified administration whim glowered admire	*Chapters 16–18* exquisite sophisticated rummaged overwhelming grimly professionally *Chapters 19–23 and Afterword* pry urgent rare puny languid serenity
Holes by Louis Sachar Farrar, Straus & Giroux	*Chapters 1–6* hovers stifling obstacle convicted descendants vast barren desolate violation prospect torment *Chapters 7–16* defective doomed deftly compacted excavated preposterous grimaced radiated intensity appropriate occasionally paranoid evict	*Chapters 17–20* throb penetrating condemned dread toxic recede writhed agony *Chapters 21–31* defiance grotesque distracted mocked humid feeble refuge urge	*Chapters 32–42* lurched accelerated random parched resist distract protruding increments contritely feebly destiny coincidence fugitive *Chapters 43–50* inexplicable abruptly distinctive adjacent precarious suppress initiate tedious subtle

Book/author/publisher	Vocabulary words		
Ida B . . . and Her Plans to Maximize Fun, Avoid Disaster, and (Possibly) Save the World by Katherine Hannigan Greenwillow	*Chapters 1–7* eternity forbearance peeved tense transformed ponder *Chapters 8–15* resolution reassurance preoccupied foe revolting vileness formulate tribulations	*Chapters 16–23* previous dilemma compromising indignant muster mourning obstacle deteriorating formidable	*Chapters 24–32* retribution mortification discreetly retaliation atonement cordial confounded perseverance
Maniac Magee by Jerry Spinelli HarperTrophy	*Chapters 1–6* legacy accurate lunging theories glared infamous clamoring emanations *Chapters 7–11* pandemonium intercepted befuddled fatal cringed prospects *Chapters 12–19* solemnly converged expired regretted publicize contortions	*Chapters 20–23* testimony grim opponent spectators calmly alertness cunning distraction flinched escort notion *Chapters 24–27* dumbfounded tempted conclusion prodded frayed robust sleazy immortality flaunting	*Chapters 28–31* climax preposterous consciousness soared proclaimed dispersing languished arrayed ventured meandering timidly *Chapters 32–35* stoic vaguely solitary careening vast desolation gaunt retaliated warily prone

Book/author/publisher	Vocabulary words		
Maniac Magee (cont.)	*Chapters 36–38* devour heroic nonchalance perilous marooned compromise consequences exuberance reprisals	*Chapters 39–43* ecstatic ludicrous sympathy extort frenzied chaotic stability enchanted random diverged	
Song of the Trees by Mildred D. Taylor Dell	vivid finicky resuming emerged	indignantly mournfully haughtily	epic elude woefully
Shiloh by Phyllis Reynolds Naylor Dell	*Chapters 1–6* groveling cringe flustered thrusting feeble tense nourish commences lean humble	*Chapters 7–15* envy remedy obliged generous mournful intention	duty evidence jubilation legal witness bond
Stone Fox by John Reynolds Gardiner Harper	official legal stunned	amateurs cunning treacherous	admire tension
The Tale of Despereaux by Kate DiCamillo Candlewick	*Chapters 1–3* ordeal speculation siblings indignant relishing destined conform	*Chapters 4–6* abandoned indulge adhere grave captivating executing affected	*Chapters 7–9* dismay protested indisputable fervent assume renounce perfidy assured

(*cont.*)

Book/author/publisher	Vocabulary words		
The Tale of Despereaux (cont.)	*Chapters 10–12* distinctive egregious regret defiance ominous burly escort flawless *Chapters 13–15* irritably frustration appropriate contemplate implications encountered ironies *Chapters 16–19* prophecy inexplicably contentment obsession despicable torment astute consigned	*Chapters 20–23* ornate spectacle revelation admiration distracted misery obvious revenge dire consequences *Chapters 24–30* inquire scrupulously crisis confidence notion permeated assured *Chapters 31–33* overwhelming stench deliberate ceased detain panic portentous aspirations diabolical	*Chapters 34–37* advanced intending pondering gratitude covert rage *Chapters 38–42* ceasing empathetic makeshift diminishment audible meditative quest *Chapters 43–47* perspective calculating beatific inspiring emboldened maneuvering devious gusto thwarted *Chapters 48–52* negotiated contemplate vengeful infringe consign sentiment anticipated fragile
The Whipping Boy by Sid Fleischman Greenwillow	defiant contrite insolent	villain arrogantly vile	elation notorious

GRADES 6–8		
Novels		
Book/author/publisher	**Vocabulary words**	
Chasing Vermeer by Blue Balliett Scholastic	*Chapters 1–6* discriminating pretentious agitated intriguing relevant sophisticated conviction exhilarating *Chapters 7–12* inexplicable ventured sinister ingenious obscurity intimidated judiciously	*Chapters 13–18* random dismal radical reminiscing conspicuous vigorously moral imperious	*Chapters 19–24* menacing overwrought valid ruthless precariously indulgently speculated eerie
The Giver by Lois Lowry Houghton Mifflin	*Chapters 1–4* ironic palpable distraught apprehensive pondered aptitude chastise remorse conviction serene *Chapters 5–8* reprieve exuberant somber meticulously prestige ruefully benign anguish	*Chapters 9–12* logistic exemption excruciating conspicuous tentatively perceived obsolete relinquished *Chapters 13–16* alien mutilated chaos subsided assimilated forsake assuage ominous	*Chapters 17–23* permeated warily dejected solace languid relentless obscured lethargy

Book/author/publisher	Vocabulary words		
Jacob Have I Loved by Katherine Paterson HarperTrophy	*Chapters 1–4* precarious avid affluent vulgar fervent petulant pretentious melancholy	*Chapters 9–12* aberrations wily undaunted consternation capricious relegated cunning placidly	*Chapters 17–20* gaudy exasperating contend taunt rancor renunciation taint desolate
	Chapters 5–8 ironic feigned zeal pretense contempt integrity futile interloper	*Chapters 13–16* adamant propriety exotic culminating exuberant destitute perfunctorily elusive	
The Outsiders by S. E. Hinton Dell	*Chapters 1–4* asset unfathomable rivalry incredulous rebellious stricken gallantly aloofness bleakly contemptuously premonition acquitted	*Chapters 5–8* imploringly sullenly eluded indignant conviction detached radiates aghast	*Chapters 9–12* mortal conformity discipline contempt agony idolized
A Wrinkle in Time by Madeleine L'Engle Dell	*Chapters 1–3* serenity vulnerable prodigious indignantly agility warily belligerent sinister tangible	*Chapters 4–6* inexorable perturbed raptly transition writhe malignant resilience vulnerable	*Chapters 7–9* bravado diverting tenacity pedantic ominous monotonous deviate distorting omnipotent miasma ruthlessly

(cont.)

Book/author/publisher	Vocabulary words	
A Wrinkle in Time (cont.)	*Chapters 10–12* atrophied fallible assuaged emanate pungent perplexity jeopardize vulnerable distraught reiterating vestige	
Short Stories		
Book/author/publisher	**Story/vocabulary words**	
A Book of Myths: Selections from Bulfinch's Age of Fable by Helen Sewell Macmillan	*Prometheus and Pandora* interposed lurked bestow sagacity prodigal noxious disdained magnanimous	*Phaeton* rustic paternal vesture novelty aspire perpetually foreboding agile torpid hapless sustain omnipotent
A Couple of Kooks and Other Stories about Love by Cynthia Rylant Orchard	*Checkouts* reverie solitary harried deftly coincided	transition tedious obsessive perverse articulate
Get Off the Unicorn by Anne McCaffrey Del Ray	*The Smallest Dragonboy* imperative imminent incredulous dissipate	ignominious consternation oblivious
The Library Card by Jerry Spinelli Scholastic	*Mongoose* swaggered baffled careened notion	vandalism meandered seething wary

Book/author/publisher	Story/vocabulary words	
A Book of Myths: Selections from Bulfinch's Age of Fable by Helen Sewell Macmillan	*Prometheus and Pandora* interposed lurked bestow sagacity prodigal noxious disdained magnanimous	*Phaeton* rustic paternal vesture novelty aspire perpetually foreboding agile torpid hapless sustain omnipotent
Three Skeleton Key by George G. Toudouze Esquire	monotonous uncanny fetid incessantly	morose seething derisive incendiary

SOME CLASSIC SHORT STORIES FOR HIGH SCHOOL READERS

Story/author	Vocabulary words	
The Fall of the House of Usher by Edgar Allan Poe	oppressively pervaded sublime malady acute pallid	solace morbid anomalous palpable succumbed paradoxical
The Lottery by Shirley Jackson	profusely boisterous jovial paraphernalia ritual	perfunctory interminably petulantly defiantly conformity (does not appear in the story)
The Minister's Black Veil by Nathaniel Hawthorne	meditative perturbation venerable iniquity melancholy	ostentatious sagacious portend obstinacy ambiguity
The Monkey's Paw by W. W. Jacobs	presumptuous talisman enthralled maligned dubiously	prosaic avaricious furtively sinister apathy

Story/author	Vocabulary words	
The Necklace by Guy de Maupassant	destiny adorned indignant exquisite seductive	chagrin disconsolate frugal ardor ironic (does not appear in the story)
An Occurrence at Owl Creek Bridge by Ambrose Bierce	sentinel deference apprehension poignant intellectual	anguish grotesque interminable malign ineffable
Paul's Case by Willa Cather	aversion contempt insolence vindictive vivacious	monotony loathing lethargy oblivion exploited
The Sniper by Liam O'Flaherty	ascetic fanatic ruse silhouetted	reeling agony remorse
The Street That Got Mislaid by Patrick Waddington	profound protracted omniscient consternation infallible	diminutive amity belligerent defied renunciation
To Build a Fire by Jack London	intangible frailty keen apprehension imperative	imperceptible excruciating devised acute endurance

References

Anders, P., Bos, C., & Filip, D. (1984). The effect of semantic feature analysis on the reading comprehension of learning-disabled students. In J. A. Niles & L. A. Harris (Eds.), *Changing perspectives on research in reading/language processing and instruction* (pp. 162–166). Rochester, NY: National Reading Conference.

Anderson, J. R., & Reder, L. M. (1979). An elaborative processing explanation of depth of processing. In L. S. Cermak & F. I. M. Craik (Eds.), *Levels of processing in human memory* (pp. 385–404). Hillsdale, NJ: Erlbaum.

Anderson, R. C., & Freebody, P. (1983). Reading comprehension and the assessment and acquisition of word knowledge. In B. Hutton (Ed.), *Advances in reading/language research: A research annual* (pp. 231–256). Greenwich, CT: JAI Press.

August, D., & Shanahan, T. (2006). *Developing literacy in second-language learners: Report of the National Literacy Panel on Language—Minority Children and Youth.* New York: Routledge.

Banks, K. (2006). *Max's words.* New York: Farrar, Straus & Giroux.

Barron, M. (2007). *The cat and the parrot: An Indian folk tale retold.* Unpublished manuscript.

Baumann, J. F., Font, G., Edwards, E. D., & Boland, E. (2005). Strategies for teaching middle-grade students to use word-part and context clues to expand reading vocabulary. In E. H. Hiebert & M. L. Kamil (Eds.), *Teaching and learning vocabulary: Bringing research to practice* (pp. 179–205). Mahwah, NJ: Erlbaum.

Baumann, J. F., Kame'enui, E. J., & Ash, G. E. (2003). Research on vocabulary instruction: Voltaire redux. In J. Flood, D. Lapp, J. R. Squire, & J. M. Jensen (Eds.), *Handbook of research on teaching the English language arts* (pp. 752–785). Mahwah, NJ: Erlbaum.

Beck, I. L., & McKeown, M. G. (2007). Increasing young low-income children's oral vocabulary repertoires through rich and focused instruction. *Elementary School Journal, 107*(3), 251–271.

Beck I. L., McKeown, M. G., & Kucan, L. (2002). *Bringing words to life: Robust vocabulary instruction.* New York: Guilford Press.

Beck, I. L., McKeown, M. G., & Omanson, R. (1987). The effects and uses of diverse vocabulary instructional techniques. In M. G. McKeown & M. E. Curtis (Eds.), *The nature of vocabulary acquisition* (pp. 147–163). Hillsdale, NJ: Erlbaum.

Beck, I. L., McKeown, M. G., Omanson, R. C., & Pople, M. T. (1984). Improving the comprehensibility of stories: The effects of revisions that improve coherence. *Reading Research Quarterly, 19*(3), 263–277.

Beck, I. L., Perfetti, C. A., & McKeown, M. G. (1982). Effects of long-term vocabulary instruction on lexical access and reading comprehension. *Journal of Educational Psychology, 74*(4), 506–521.

Biemiller, A. (1999, April). *Estimating vocabulary growth for ESL children with and without listening comprehension instruction.* Paper presented at the annual conference of the American Educational Research Association, Montreal, Quebec.

Blachowicz, C. L. Z., Fisher, P. J. L., Ogle, D., & Watts-Taffe, S. (2006). Vocabulary: Questions from the classroom. *Reading Research Quarterly, 41*(4), 524–539.

Blachowicz, C. L. Z., & Obrochta, C. (2005). Vocabulary visits: Virtual field trips for content vocabulary development. *The Reading Teacher, 59*(3), 262–268.

Blake, R. K. (2007). *The tailor: A folk tale retold.* Unpublished manuscript.

Bolger, D. J., Balass, M., Landen, E. & Perfetti, C. A. (in press). Contextual variation and definitions in learning the meaning of words. *Discourse Processes.*

Bond, M. A., & Wasik, B. A. (2007). *Conversation stations: Promoting language in early childhood classrooms.* Manuscript submitted for publication.

Calderon, M., August, D., Slavin, R., Duran, D., Madden, N., & Cheung, A. (2005). Bringing words to life in classrooms with English-language learners. In A. H. Hiebert & M. L. Kamil (Eds.), *Teaching and learning vocabulary* (pp. 113–138). Mahwah, NJ: Erlbaum.

Calmenson, S., & Sutcliff, J. (1998). *Rosie: A visiting dog's story.* New York: Clarion Books.

Cameron, A. (1989). *The stories Julian tells.* New York: Dell Yearling.

Carlisle, J. F. (2007). Fostering morphological processing, vocabulary development, and reading comprehension. In R. K. Wagner, A. E. Muse, & K. R. Tannenbaum (Eds.), *Vocabulary acquisition: Implications for reading comprehension* (pp. 78–103). New York: Guilford Press.

Carroll, J. B., Davies, P., & Richman, B. (1971). *Word frequency book.* New York: American Heritage.

Catts, H. W., Fey, M. E., Zhang, X., & Tomblin, B. (1999). Language basis of reading and reading disabilities: Evidence from a longitudinal investigation. *Scientific Studies of Reading, 3*(4), 331–361.

Cleary, B. (1984). *Ramona forever.* New York: HarperCollins.

Clough, S. (2005, May). The wisdom of goats. *Cricket Magazine,* pp. 10–14.

Corson, D. J. (1985). *The lexical bar.* Oxford, UK: Pergamon Press.

Corson, D. J. (1995). *Using English words,* Dordrecht, The Netherlands: Kluwer Academic.

Coxhead, A. (1998). *An academic word list* (Occasional Publication No. 18). Wellington, New Zealand: Victoria University of Wellington.

Craik, F. I. M., & Tulving, E. (1975). Depth of processing and the retention of words in episodic memory. *Journal of Experimental Psychology: General, 104,* 268–294.

Culham, R. (2003). *6 + 1 traits of writing: The complete guide grades 3 and up.* New York: Scholastic.

Cummins, J. (1994). The acquisition of English as a second language. In K. Spangenberg-Urbschat & R. Pritchard (Eds.), *Kids come in all languages: Reading instruction for ESL students* (pp. 36–62). Newark, DE: International Reading Association.

Cunningham, A. E., & Stanovich, K. E. (1997). Early reading acquisition and its relation to reading experience and ability 10 years later. *Developmental Psychology, 33*(6), 934–945.

Curtis, C. P. (1995). *The Watsons go to Birmingham—1963.* New York: Bantam Doubleday Dell Books for Young Readers.

Curtis, M. E. (1987). Vocabulary testing and instruction. In M. G. McKeown & M. E. Curtis (Eds.), *The nature of vocabulary acquisition* (pp. 37–51). Hillsdale, NJ: Erlbaum.

Curtis, M. E. (2006). The role of vocabulary instruction in adult basic education. In J. Comings, B. Garner, & C. Smith (Eds.), *Review of adult learning and literacy* (Vol. 6, pp. 43–69). Mahwah, NJ: Erlbaum.

Dale, E., & Chall, J. S. (1948). A formula for predicting readability. *Educational Research Bulletin, 27,* 37–54.

Darling-Hammond, L., & Cobb, V. L. (1996). The changing context of teacher education. In F. B. Murray (Ed.), *The teacher educator's handbook* (pp. 14–62). San Francisco: Jossey-Bass.

Davis, F. B. (1944). Fundamental factors in reading comprehension. *Psychometrika, 9,* 185–197.

Delacroix, L., et al. (Eds.). (2007). *Longman advanced American dictionary* (2nd ed.). Edinburgh, UK: Pearson Education Limited.

Dickinson, E. (1997). "Hope" is the thing with feathers. Available online at rpo.library.utoronto.ca/poem/633.html. Original work published 1891.

Dole, J. A., & Osborn, J. (2004). Professional development for K–3 teachers: Content and process. In D. S. Strickland & M. L. Kamil (Eds.), *Improving reading achievement through professional development* (pp. 65–74). Norwood, MA: Christopher–Gordon.

Duin, A. H., & Graves, M. F. (1987). Intensive vocabulary instruction as a prewriting technique. *Reading Research Quarterly, 22,* 311–330.

Dunn, L., & Dunn, L. (1997). *Peabody Picture Vocabulary Test—Third Edition.* Circle Pines, MN: American Guidance Services.

Durkin, D. (1978–1979). What classroom observations reveal about reading comprehension instruction. *Reading Research Quarterly, 14,* 481–533.

Dutro, S., & Moran, C. (2003). Rethinking English language instruction: An architectural approach. In G. Garcia (Ed.), *English learners: Reaching the highest level of English literacy* (pp. 227–258). Newark, DE: International Reading Association.

Elmore, R. F. (2002). *Bridging the gap between standards and achievement.* Washington, DC: Albert Shanker Institute.

Farr, R. C., Strickland, D. S., & Beck, I. L. (2001). *Collections: A Harcourt reading/language arts program.* Orlando, FL: Harcourt.

Gaines, E. P. (2001, March). Aquatic guests. *Cricket,* 48–53.

Gamarra, P. (1993). The bridge on the river Clarinette. In J. Barry, S. Siamon, & G. Huser (Eds.), *Just fantastic!* (pp. 100–104). Calgary, Canada: Nelson Canada.

Garg, A. (2007). A.Word.A.Day website. *wordsmith.org/awad/index.html.*

Graves, M. F. (2006). *The vocabulary book: Learning and instruction.* New York: Teachers College Press.

Hart, B., & Risley, T. R. (1999). The social world of children learning to talk. Baltimore: Brookes.

Hayes, D. P., & Ahrens, M. G. (1988). Vocabulary simplification for children: A special case of "motherese"? *Journal of Child Language, 15,* 395–410.

Hurwitz, J. (1984). *The hot and cold summer.* New York: Scholastic.

Johnson, D. D., & Pearson, P. D. (1978). *Teaching reading vocabulary.* New York: Holt, Rinehart & Winston.

Johnson, D. D., & Pearson, P. D. (1984). *Teaching reading vocabulary* (2nd ed.). New York: Holt, Rinehart & Winston.

Kame'enui, E. J., Carnine, D. W., & Freschi, R. (1982). Effects of text construction and instructional procedures for teaching word meanings on comprehension and recall. *Reading Research Quarterly, 17,* 367–388.

Kindler, A. L. (2002). *Survey of the states' limited English proficient students and available educational programs and services* (2000–2001 Summary Report). Washington, DC: National Clearinghouse for English Language Acquisition.

Konigsburg, E. L. (1998). *The view from Saturday.* New York: Aladdin.

Kowal, M., & Swain, M. (1994). Using collaborative language production tasks to promote students' language awareness. *Language Awareness, 3,* 73–93.

Kucan, L., Trathen, W. R., & Straits, W. J. (2007). A professional development initiative for developing approaches to vocabulary instruction with secondary mathematics, art, science, and English teachers. *Reading Research and Instruction, 46,* (2), 175–195.

MacLachlan, P. (1985). *Sarah, plain and tall.* New York: HarperCollins.

Margosein, C. M., Pascarella, E. T., & Pflaum, S. W. (1982, April). *The effects of instruction using semantic mapping on vocabulary and comprehension.* Paper presented at the annual meeting of the American Educational Research Association, New York.

McKeown, M. G. (1993). Creating effective definitions for young word learners. *Reading Research Quarterly, 28,* 16–31.

McKeown, M. G., Beck, I. L., Omanson, R. C., & Perfetti, C. A. (1983). The effects of long-term vocabulary instruction on reading comprehension: A replication. *Journal of Reading Behavior, 15*(1), 3–18.

McKeown, M. G., Beck, I. L., Omanson, R. C., & Pople, M. T. (1985). Some effects of the nature and frequency of vocabulary instruction on the knowledge and use of words. *Reading Research Quarterly, 20*(5), 522–535.

McMillan, B. (1997). *Night of the pufflings.* New York: Houghton Mifflin.

Mezynski, K. (1983). Issues concerning the acquisition of knowledge: Effects of vocabulary training on reading comprehension. *Review of Educational Research, 53,* 253–279.

Moseley, D. S. (2004). Vocabulary instruction and its effects on writing quality. *Dissertation Abstracts International, A: The Humanities and Social Sciences, 64*(8), 2767-A.

Namioka, L. (1995). *Yang the third and her impossible family.* New York: Bantam Doubleday Dell Books for Young Readers.

Nation, I. S. P. (2001). *Learning vocabulary in another language.* Cambridge, UK: Cambridge University Press.

Nation, P. (1990). *Teaching and learning vocabulary.* New York: Newbury House.

National Reading Panel. (2000). *Teaching children to read: An evidence-based assessment of the scientific research literature on reading and its implications for reading instruction.* Washington, DC: National Institute of Child Health and Human Development.

Nichols, C. N. (2007). *The effects of three methods of introducing vocabulary to elementary students: Traditional, friendly definitions, and parsing.* Unpublished doctoral dissertation, University of Pittsburgh, Pittsburgh.

O'Connor, J. (2000). *Fancy Nancy and the posh puppy.* New York: HarperCollins.

Paulsen, G. (1987). *Hatchet.* New York: Atheneum Books for Young Readers.

Pickett, Joseph P., et al. (Eds.). (2000). *The American Heritage dictionary of the English language* (4th ed.). Boston: Houghton Mifflin. Available online at *http://www.bartleby.com/61/*

Plume, I. (1998). *The Bremen-town musicians.* New York: Dragonfly Books.

Poe, E. A. (1984). The oval portrait. In *Complete stories and poems of Edgar Allan Poe* (pp. 568–570). New York: Doubleday.

Poe, E. A. (1984). The tell tale heart. *In Complete stories and poems of Edgar Allan Poe* (pp. 121–124). New York: Doubleday.

Roth, F. P., Speece, D. L., & Cooper, D. H. (2002). A longitudinal analysis of the connection between oral language and early reading. *Journal of Educational Research, 95*(5), 259–272.

Ryder, R. J., & Graves, M. E. (1994). Vocabulary instruction presented prior to reading in two basal readers. *Elementary School Journal, 95*(2), 139–153.

Schotter, R. (2006). *The boy who loved words.* New York: Schwartz & Wade.

Scott, J., & Nagy, W. E. (1990). *Definitions: Understanding students' misunderstandings.* Paper presented at the annual meeting of the American Educational Research Association, Boston, MA.

Scott, J. A., Jamieson-Noel, D., & Asselin, M. (2003). Vocabulary instruction throughout the day in twenty-three Canadian upper-elementary classrooms. *Elementary School Journal, 103,*(3), 269–312.

Scott, J. A., Skobel, B. J., & Wells, J. W. (2008). *The word-conscious classroom: Building the vocabulary readers and writers need.* New York: Scholastic.

Sinclair, J., et al. (Eds.). (1987). *Collins COBUILD dictionary: English language.* London: Collins.

Singer, H. (1965). A developmental model of speed of reading in grade 3 through 6. *Reading Research Quarterly, 1,* 29–49.

Snicket, L. (2000). *The austere academy.* New York: HarperCollins.

Snicket, L. (2001a). *The ersatz elevator.* New York: HarperCollins.

Snicket, L. (2001b). *The hostile hospital.* New York: HarperCollins.

Snicket, L. (2001c). *The vile village.* New York: HarperCollins.

Snow, C. E., Tabors, P. O., Nicholson, P. A., & Kurland, B. F. (1995). SHELL: Oral language and early literacy skills in kindergarten and first-grade children. *Journal of Research in Childhood Education, 10,* 37–47.

Spearrit, D. (1972). Identification of subskills of reading comprehension by maximum likelihood factor analysis. *Reading Research Quarterly, 8,* 92–111.

Stahl, S. A., & Fairbanks, M. M. (1986). The effects of vocabulary instruction: A model-based meta-analysis. *Review of Educational Research, 56,* 72–110.

Stahl, S. A., & Nagy, W. E. (2006). *Teaching word meanings.* Mahwah, NJ: Erlbaum.

Steig, W. (1982). *Doctor DeSoto.* New York: Farrar, Straus & Giroux.

Strickland, D. S., Kamil, M. L., Walberg, H. J., & Manning, J. B. (2004). Reports and recommendations from the National Invitational Conference "Improving Reading through Professional Development." In D. S. Strickland & M. L. Kamil (Eds.), *Improving reading achievement through professional development* (pp. vii–xi). Norwood, MA: Christopher–Gordon.

Thurstone, L. L. (1946). A note on a re-analysis of Davis' reading tests. *Psychometrika, 11,* 185–188.

Van Allsburg, C. (1984). *The mysteries of Harris Burdick.* Providence, RI: Houghton Mifflin.

Wagner, R. K., Torgeson, J. K., Rashotte, C. A., Hecht, S. A., Barker, T. A., Burgess, S. R., et al. (1997). Changing relations between phonological processing abilities and word-level reading as children develop from beginning to skilled readers: A 5-year longitudinal study. *Developmental Psychology, 33,* 468–479.

Walsh, K. (2003). Basal readers: The lost opportunity to build the knowledge that propels comprehension. *American Educator, 21*(1), 24–27.

West, M. (1953). *A general service list of English words.* London: Longman, Green & Co.

White, E. B. (1952). *Charlotte's web.* New York: Harper & Row.

White, T., Sowell, J., & Yanagihara,A. (1989). Teaching elementary students to use word-part clues. *The Reading Teacher, 42,* 302–308.

Word Central: Merriam–Webster's student's electronic dictionary. (2007, August). Website at *http://www.m-w.com/dictionary.htm.*

Zeno, S. M., Ivens, S. H., Millard, R. T., & Duvvuri, R. (1995). *The educator's word frequency guide.* New York: Touchstone Applied Science Associates.

Index